PATOUT'S
CAJUN
HOME
COOKING

Patout's Cajun Home Cooking

ALEX PATOUT

Photographs by Glade Bilby

Random House New York

Library of Congress Cataloging-in-Publication Data

Patout, Alex, 1952–
Patout's Cajun home cooking.

Includes index.
1. Cookery, American—Louisiana style. I. Title.
II. Title: Cajun home cooking.
TX715.P3168 1986   641.59763   86-10239
ISBN 0-394-54725-X

Manufactured in the United States of America

23456789
First Edition

BOOK DESIGN BY LILLY LANGOTSKY

Dedicated to the prior three generations,
who helped make it all possible

Eugenie Pellerin Arnandez,
my paternal great grandmother
(1871–1946)

Yvonne Arnandez Patout Southwell ("MoMo"),
my paternal grandmother
(1896–   )

Elva Jeansonne Bolner ("Maw Maw"),
my maternal grandmother
(1900–1977)

and my parents

Eugene Alexander Patout, Sr.
(1925–   )

Ann Bolner Patout
(1931–   )

ACKNOWLEDGMENTS

To the total dedication of my brothers and sisters, without whose efforts and performance the Patout family enterprise could not have grown: Eugenie ("Gigi"), Andre, Liz, and Mitch.

CONTENTS

INTRODUCTION

These days, you can find "Cajun" on menus from Portland, Oregon, to Portland, Maine. But most people's—even most food-lovers'—acquaintance with the term doesn't extend much beyond the bowl of "Cajun popcorn" next to their elbows at their favorite watering holes.

To discover what Cajun is all about, it's important first to know who the Cajuns are. Today's Cajuns live within the area of southwestern Louisiana known as Acadiana, which runs from fifty miles west of New Orleans to the western border of the state, and from as far north as Avolleyes Parish (a little below the middle of the state) to the Gulf of Mexico. This region has a distinct heritage that is alive and well today—in its customs, its art, its music, and, above all, its cuisine. Cajun music has moved from the backroom bars of southwestern Louisiana all the way to the Grammy Awards (Clifton Chenier in 1985, and Chez Sidney—for "Don't Mess with My Tutu"—in 1986) and Carnegie Hall (Beaujolais with Mike Doucette). Premier Cajun artist George Rodrigue shows his work all over the United States and abroad, and in such folk arts as woodcarving, we lead the country. Even the Smithsonian has had Cajun on display. But perhaps the biggest landmark of all was the Cajun dinner prepared under the direction of Paul Prudhomme for the heads of state at President Reagan's Williamsburg summit in 1983. That's a long way to come from the bayous and swamps of Acadiana!

The land along the bayous of present-day Cajun country was settled by the Spanish and the French, but it was the Acadians—descendants of southern French farmers who had emigrated to Nova Scotia in the early 1600s and who migrated southward after being driven out by the British a century later—who were the area's real first colonists. Only a fraction of them survived the long trek down to New Orleans, but from there they settled along the bayous to the west and resumed their usual livelihoods—farming, fishing, and trapping. They had little education or money; they had to survive on what they could grow, catch, or trap. They had brought with them as much as they could carry, and one of the things they carried was their way of life, which meant perhaps above all their way of cooking. Something that was already a part of their culinary tradition was the flair they had developed along the North Atlantic for applying the old familiar country-style methods to a completely new environment.

So the Cajuns weren't inclined to be intimidated by this strange new land with its strange new animals and plants—even okra, which slaves had brought with them from Africa. They were quick to assimilate the spicy influences of Spanish cooking, too—and the even spicier uses to which the Indians put the abundant peppers—while they went about applying their magical French roux and country habit of long, slow cooking to every ingredient in sight. And so from the beginning Cajun was not just one people with one tradition, but rather a tradition of adaptation and innovation that persists in Cajun to this day.

The wealthier French and Spanish who governed Louisiana by turns and were concentrated in New Orleans knew something about innovation, too. So did their cooks, who were mostly black, and who had to switch their culinary styles from French to Spanish and back again, to please the ruling palates of the day. Naturally, elements carried over from one regime to the next, so that by the turn of the nineteenth century, the distinct French and Spanish culinary styles had converged into a new cuisine—Creole. The term came to refer as well to those Louisianians who were descended from the Spanish or French, as opposed to the newcomers who were flooding into the state from other parts of the country. By this time, New Orleans had become a major center of commerce.

In fact, by 1850, half the millionaires in the United States lived or had property in New Orleans or along the river. And as it became a metropolis, it also developed into one of the world's culinary capitals. Not only did it feature elaborate food in private homes, it also boasted some of the finest restaurants to be found—a few, like Antoine's, still in operation today.

But one hundred miles to the west, a small but intense culture quite apart from all this urban bustle was growing. The Cajuns had no good system of communication among themselves, let alone with the city, and not much occasion for socializing—there was too much hard work to be done. Recipes for the hearty, spicy fare that kept them on their feet from one end of the day to the other were handwritten if they were written at all. Cooking was a private art in a culture where art was a precious luxury, and secrets of the kitchen were jealousy guarded. Even basic recipes varied from one family to the next, and from one generation to the next within a given household. By the time grandmother's gumbo got to granddaughter, it was completely transformed—because mother had held back some trademark secret, no doubt. The point is that what developed along the bayous was a home-style cuisine with no hard and fast rules, from gumbo to jambalaya to sauce piquante.

But who were the Patouts, and what made them so unique—and such especially great cooks in a land of great cooks? The original Louisiana Patout was Simeon, who came to Louisiana with his wife directly from France in 1828. They were given a land grant of four thousand acres to set up a vineyard. They tried to grow grapes for a number of years, but their crop wasn't compatible with the Louisiana climate and soil, and they abandoned it in favor of sugarcane by 1840. In fact, Patouts still operate the oldest existing sugar plantation in the country, in Patoutville, outside New Iberia. But my great-grandfather Felix sold out his interest in the sugar plantation and moved to New Iberia—a small town, but it seemed big to him. He set up several businesses there, among them a hotel, which he named The Frederic after his son, my grandfather. Frederic married Yvonne Arnandez, who had a tremendous knowledge of food. Her mother, a Pellerin, had a collection of more than a hundred handwritten recipes from her family. Some of the recipes in this book—especially in the Pickles and Preserves and Sweets chapters—are hers. Frederic and Yvonne had eight children and were relatively well-to-do, which allowed them greater luxuries at the table than most Cajun families could afford. My father, their fifth child, earned a degree in hotel and restaurant management. After working in hotels across the country, he returned to New Iberia in the early 1950s, where with his brother Gerald he operated a restaurant at the hotel—one of the first to bring Cajun home-style food out of private kitchens. The restaurant flourished for a number of years, but by the end of the 1960s, the intrusion of the interstate highway system and the growth of the motel business had made it virtually impossible for such hotels to survive. So Daddy left the restaurant business to become an insurance agent and continued cooking strictly for enjoyment, at home and at his fishing and hunting camps.

As for me, I never realized how good the food was that I grew up with until I began to eat out with friends in Lafayette. Commercial food was terrible. But when I brought my friends home to dinner with my family, I still didn't quite understand why their eyes lit up so. Daddy, with his years of experience in commercial kitchens, did. I was cocky enough, though, to believe that eating so well at home made me something of a food expert at age twenty-five, though I didn't cook much growing up and had never worked a day in a kitchen in my life. And so I decided to open a restaurant. Since I had a degree in accounting from the University of Southwestern Louisiana, I was able to put together a performance statement that the bank and investors felt comfortable with. Then I told my idea to my sister Gigi, who was skeptical until we sat down and worked out a plan we were both excited about. Our announcement to the family was greeted with all the enthusiasm that greeted the atom bomb. My father wouldn't speak to me for two weeks, though Mama was a bit more understanding. Daddy came around, however, and we opened in November 1979.

But four months after we opened, work began on the two-lane highway that ran in front of the restaurant, to widen it to five lanes. The construction lasted a year and nine months, and our business dropped from the break-even point to nearly a standstill. Four of my father's friends stepped in and bought the building and the property from us, putting us on a gradual rent program that began at zero for the first six months. We cut our payroll to Gigi, me, and two other staff members. But we managed to stay open noon and night, six days a week. I ran the kitchen, with the help of a dishwasher whom I taught to fry; Gigi, with the help of one waitress, ran the front, acting as hostess, cashier, bartender, and busgirl. Thank God, that didn't last very long. As business grew, we added one person to the payroll at a time, as we could afford it and as business demanded.

While business was slow, though, I had a lot of time to think. And the more I thought, the more I began to rethink everything, from the ground up. I remembered my original concept of the restaurant, and everything I'd wanted it to be, and I began to walk into the restaurant each day thinking, "There must me something I can change today that will make one dish that much better than it was yesterday." I was prepared to start from scratch. I even let Daddy come into the kitchen to show me how to make a simple crab dressing—a basic recipe that we haven't changed in the four years since. In fact, we even call it Crab Eugen. I began to realize that my greatest strength was the experiences and standards that growing up a Patout had given me. And as we started to grow again, that attitude—that confidence—took hold not just in my immediate family, but in the staff as well.

It was through the help of a close friend, Joe Cahn, that Patout's began to be known beyond the immediate area. Joe and his wife, Karen, ran the New Orleans School of Cooking (they still do). We were both fans of Frank Davis, the highly vocal and often hilarious DJ whose Saturday show on WWL radio in New Orleans was so popular that people all over the southeastern United States (his listening area) would do their household chores during the week so that they'd have Saturdays free to listen to "Weekend Alive." Frank had a tremendous sense not only of what was natural to New Orleans, but of what was in the heart of every south Louisianian, from the Pearl River to the Sabine Pass. Paul Prudhomme cooked with him frequently over the air. Joe suggested that I bring Frank some food—he could arrange it, no problem. So I loaded up my pickup truck with Redfish Courtbouillon, Shrimp Creole, and Crawfish Yvonne at about seven o'clock one Saturday morning and headed for New Orleans. I arrived at Joe's place at about half past eleven, which is when I realized that he hadn't made call one. I wondered if he even *knew* Frank. But I decided there was no use worrying about it, and I started warming up the food. Meanwhile, Joe was calling the station every five minutes and getting a busy signal. At about half past one, he got through. Fortunately, if there's anything true about Frank Davis, it's that he's never turned down a free meal in his life, so when Joe told him he had a young chef from southwest Louisiana standing by with hot food, waiting to be told what to do next, Frank wanted to know how come I wasn't on my way to the station. Next thing I knew, I was face to face with this amazing human being who was sitting in front of a mike, saying, "Hi, I'm Frank. What you got to eat?" I said, "Hi, I'm Alex Patout, from Patout's Restaurant in New Iberia." I proceeded to set out the food, and all I remember him saying is, "Mmmm, this is wonderful. Now remember, this is live over the radio. You go ahead and talk." So I talked, told all about who I was and where I was from, what I'd brought and how it was made, and Frank just kept handing back empty dishes and saying, "Mmmm, this is good. You just go ahead and talk, boy." I stayed on the air with him for forty-five minutes.

I called Frank the next week to thank him, and to offer my services as a contact for happenings in the bayou country. He called me his "Cajun Connection," and I was on about every other week from then on, over the telephone. Pretty soon, we had people dropping into the restaurant from all over the southeastern United States, saying, "I heard you on Frank Davis's show and I had to come see what you were all about."

This new popularity finally gave me the confidence to approach the one person I was completely in awe of, the youngest of a family of thirteen from a small town forty miles north of New Iberia—Paul Prudhomme. His warmth and openness on our first meeting banished all my nervousness, and it didn't stop there. Sometimes I'd call him up and he'd share recipes for dishes that we'd run as that evening's special, based on what I had fresh in my cooler. More important, though, he taught me to think creatively about food—to think of other ways of doing things besides the accepted ones. And above all, he taught me the importance of freshness.

He also gave me the chance to show my stuff to a lot of the

food writers who were coming to Louisiana in search of the new regional cooking. Those writers were astonished to discover two completely different cuisines—Cajun and Creole—within the same state, and amazed at the enormous variations within Cajun cuisine from locale to locale. What they were discovering was a cuisine with few set guidelines or practices—a cuisine based primarily on *taste*. Each gumbo tasted a little different from the one a little farther down the bayou, and all of them had a flavor unmatched by any other regional cooking.

A third kind of cooking has grown up in Louisiana over the past few years—a development I feel honored to have been part of. It's a cuisine that selects and marries the best that Louisiana has to offer, and it's known, appropriately enough, as Louisiana cooking. No state matches Louisiana in its abundance of fresh seafood, and the game in the marshes of the south is a hunter's paradise. Add to that the amazing variety of produce we grow, and three hundred years' mingling of French, Spanish, African, and Indian influences, and you'll understand what Cajuns know so well: Culinary innovation is simply an extension of the concepts of family and tradition. And the process never ends, because every day gives a new answer to the question "Isn't there a new, a different, a better way I can cook?"

The more immediate purpose of this book, though, is to give you the basics of Cajun home-style cooking in the truest sense—as they have been passed on from generation to generation in southern Louisiana. I hope it will not only teach you techniques and styles that you can incorporate into your everyday cooking, but also that it will instill in you a spirit of creativity in using the best and freshest of what is indigenous to *your* area. You're cooking Cajun—you're cooking Louisiana—if you're cooking with our spirit and our style. Master the basics of Cajun cooking and discover how much opens up to you beyond this book. Finally, remember that in Cajun country, good food and good times go hand in hand. So *laissez les bon temps rouler, cher!*

Basics

Home-style Cajun cooking boils down to a few essential themes and techniques, and they all have in common one aim: to feed a great many with a very little, and to feed them very well.

Roux

Many old Cajun recipes begin, "First, you take a roux . . ." Well, what exactly is a roux? A roux is simply a browning of flour in fat or oil. In classical French cooking it's flour cooked in butter just enough to get the raw taste out. In Cajun cooking it's something else again. Most Americans know roux only as the basis for a white sauce (béchamel), but for something that delicate I prefer a straight cream reduction. Cajuns cook their flour in oil until it turns a nutty brown or darker, and in the process make a base that does tricks their seventeenth-century French country cousins knew all about. It acts as a thickener of stocks and other liquids, thereby extending food to feed more people. But unlike many extenders, it adds flavor, too—a wonderful, dark taste that plays up spices and the natural sweetness of vegetables and meats. Finally, it adds color, to complement and contrast with other ingredients. A well-matched roux makes a dish both taste and look richer, and its darkness varies with the flavors and colors of everything else that goes into the pot. Cajun home-style cooking uses three different shades of roux: peanut-butter, medium, and dark, from light to dark (see the illustrations for a photograph of each). Roux the color of peanut butter is used with crawfish, for example—it highlights their beautiful golden-red color and delicate taste. Medium-colored roux is best for other kinds of seafood; it also makes a perfect base to which other ingredients can be added, after which the roux is cooked on through and ends up very dark, as in courtbouillons and sauce piquante. Dark roux is used in gumbos and chicken stews. Once you understand what roux does, you'll be able to pick the right one for your own creations.

There are as many stories about making roux as there are methods for it. We like to joke about a family member (she shall remain nameless) who is known to take the phone off the hook and lock the doors while making roux, so as not to be distracted in any way until the process is completed. If it's a special roux for a special holiday meal, she'll even park the car around the corner to make people think she's not at home.

Up until even my parents' day, roux was cooked over very low heat and for a long, long time. Wood-burning stoves and early-model ranges were harder to control, and great care had to be taken to avoid burning the roux. With modern gas or electric ranges, though, the process is much easier—and a good deal quicker. It's even been rumored lately along the bayou that roux has been cooked in the microwave—in fact, I'll tell you how (it's about as slow as the way my grandparents did it, but it doesn't have to be tended much). But before you try any shortcuts, you should master a basic roux.

❧ BASIC ROUX ☙

2 cups high-grade vegetable oil   *3–3½ cups all-purpose flour*

Place the oil in a large heavy skillet over medium heat. Heat it to about 350°F. You don't need to use a thermometer, just this simple test: Drop in a bit of flour. It should float and begin to sizzle away immediately. If the oil starts to smoke, it is too hot—remove from heat and let the temperature reduce, then proceed. Using a wooden spoon or a whisk, quickly stir in 3 cups of flour all at once, being careful not to splatter yourself. Once the flour is thoroughly mixed in, check the consistency: It should form a smooth paste that is neither runny nor clumpy or grainy. Since the absorbency of flour varies greatly, as does the body of oils, it is impossible to give an exact proportion of flour to oil—after a while you'll be able to guess with greater accuracy. (We don't even measure.) If the roux is too thin, stir in a bit more flour; if it is too thick, stir in a little oil until it reaches the proper consistency. With the roux still over medium heat, stir continuously, being sure to scrape the sides and bottom of the pot. The flour will slowly begin to brown. Simply continue to cook and stir until it reaches the desired stage of doneness. *Peanut-butter-colored roux* (which looks just like it sounds) will take 20–30 minutes. A *medium* roux will take 30–45 minutes—it should be a solid medium brown with a hint of gold in it. A *dark* roux will take 50–70 minutes. It should be dark brown, but not black. Judge your roux's doneness by the color, not the time, which will vary according to your equipment and ingredients. When it has reached the desired color, remove it from the heat and let it cool. The pot will still be very hot, so to keep the roux from cooking much more or from burning, stir it every few minutes until it is has cooled enough to arrest the cooking process. As it continues to cool, some oil will inevitably separate out around the edges and on top. Don't worry about this—when the roux has cooled completely, simply pour off any excess oil. (I like to go ahead and add a little chopped onion, bell pepper, and celery—about a cup in all—to a dark roux, even over and above the ingredients called for in the rest of the recipe, to arrest its cooking immediately and to add additional flavor.) Many recipes, such as for Shrimp and Crab Stew, courtbouillon, and sauce piquante, call for tomato or tomato sauce to be added to the roux, which is then cooked through to an almost blue-black stage. In these recipes, be sure to let your roux cool down first, then stir in the tomatoes, bring up the heat again, and cook it on through.

It is possible to make your roux in advance, for convenience (all the recipes in this book give instructions for using ready-made roux, though of course you can also make it fresh). In fact, I keep a pan of each in the cabinet, in case I need just a tablespoon for a gravy or sauce. Given its low bacteria content, roux can be stored at room temperature, but I recommend pouring it into a jar or container, covering it with a lid, foil, or plastic wrap, and storing it in the refrigerator. It will keep up to two weeks (one week if you have added vegetables to it). You can multiply the recipe as needed. You can halve it, too (in which case you should cook it in a smaller skillet—the roux should cover the entire bottom), but don't divide it smaller than that.

There is a faster method of making roux, which was developed by Paul Prudhomme to save time in commercial kitchens. Before you try it, you should be sure that you have mastered the basic technique, though, because it is harder to control the consistency or cooking process using this method.

❦ QUICK ROUX ❧

Place the flour in a large plastic bowl that is easy to handle. Place the oil in a large heavy skillet over very high heat. Once it has begun to smoke heavily, whisk in a little flour—you must use a whisk for this method, because a spoon will not break up the lumps fast enough. The flour will begin to brown immediately. Continue to add flour. The idea is to control the temperature of the oil, and therefore the darkness to which the flour cooks as it hits the oil, with the rate at which the flour is added: The faster you add the flour, the less the flour will cook. So for a peanut-butter-colored roux you'll be adding the flour a lot faster than for a dark roux. Once the roux has reached the desired color—using this method, any color will take only about 10 minutes—remove it from the heat and cool as described above.

❧ MICROWAVE ROUX ❧

Place the oil in a large microwave-proof bowl. Place it in a microwave oven set on high for about 10 minutes—until a bit of flour dropped in sizzles. Stir in the flour and continue to microwave at medium setting, stirring every 3–4 minutes. Peanut-butter-colored roux will take 20–30 minutes, medium 40–45 minutes, dark 60–70 minutes. Note: It is very important to use the largest bowl your microwave will hold, because the roux will rise as it microwaves until the flour has reached its cooking temperature.

Stocks

The second most important element in Cajun cooking is stock, which in countless dishes is mixed with roux to create the rich base for a dish. Most people shy away from making stock without giving it a chance to show how easy and worthwhile it is. But the reason stock is a mainstay of every serious cuisine is simply that it works. The flavor that a good stock gives to gumbos, courtbouillons, sauce piquantes, and countless other soups and sauces cannot be achieved with water or with inferior stock. After all, what is a gumbo but 90 percent stock? In recipes where meat, game, or poultry is cooked with water and seasonings slowly for a long time to get it nice and tender, what you're actually doing is making stock as you make the dish. But in a Redfish Courtbouillon, for example, where it is necessary to cook the fish very briefly to preserve its delicate flavor and texture, it is essential that you have a full-bodied stock at the outset, because the cooking process itself will not provide it. And when you discover how easy it is to make stock for Cajun food, you'll find yourself using good homemade stock in all your other daily cooking as well. Furthermore, stock makes perfect sense economically—it puts to use all the perfectly fresh ingredients that would otherwise have to be thrown away: meat shanks, chicken backs, shrimp peelings, fish heads, crab claws or bodies, turkey necks—the list is endless. Simply place them in a large stockpot with a couple of carrots and onions, cover with water, and bring to a boil over medium-high heat. Skim off any foam or debris, reduce the heat to low, and let simmer for a couple of hours while you do housework, read, or watch television. Just stop by every now and then to give it a stir and skim it. The aroma it will give your house is worth it alone. When your stock is finished, remove it from the heat and let it cool to room temperature. Then transfer it to plastic containers (jars are all right for the refrigerator but not for the freezer). I've even known cooks who freeze shrimp stock in ice cube trays and pop out a cube or two when they feel a dish needs a little extra flavor. Meat stocks tend to keep longer than fish or chicken stocks, but any of them will keep for several days in the refrigerator, and for months in the freezer.

In the recipes in this book, I have indicated where water is an acceptable substitute for stock, but please remember that a good stock is always preferable. And once you get in the habit of making stock, you'll find yourself shopping and cooking with it in mind—buying chicken backs on sale, setting aside rather than throwing away onion tops or carrot tops. Stock is fun, not hard work, a natural way of feeling creative and good about making the most of what you have.

Rice

Most cuisines have some starch they rely upon. For Cajuns, it's long-grain rice, which southwestern Louisiana produces a lot of.

It's said that a true Cajun can sit on the edge of a rice field and tell you exactly how much gravy it will take to cover it. A lot of people, though, are unnecessarily afraid of cooking rice. If you're one of them, here's an almost foolproof method.

☙ FOOLPROOF STEAMED RICE ❧

Pour as much raw rice as you intend to cook into a good-size saucepan with a tight-fitting lid. Add a little salt and a dash of white vinegar (it makes the rice nice and white). Cover with water to two inches or so above the rice—don't worry about being exact. Bring to a boil over medium-high heat and let the water boil away until it has fallen just below the rice line. Then reduce the heat as low as possible, cover the rice, and let it cook 10 minutes (15 if you are making a lot) without lifting the cover. Turn off the heat and let the rice sit 15–20 minutes. Don't peek! Just before serving, lift the cover and fluff up the rice with a fork. I guarantee that this method will work for you every time.

Peppers

You'll notice as you thumb through this book that certain ingredients are mainstays of Cajun cooking, especially the constant threesome—ground red or cayenne, white, and black peppers. These are used to enhance the flavors of a dish, not to dominate it, and each pepper stimulates different taste buds to this end. The black pepper hits you in the front of the mouth, the red in the back, and the white in the throat. I've tried to give amounts that will encourage people not accustomed to spicy foods to discover the magic of peppers. As you get accustomed to them, you may find yourself wanting to increase the dose. And I hope you begin to experiment with them in the rest of your daily cooking as well.

Smothering

This violent-sounding term refers to one of the most common Cajun cooking techniques—one of the first I learned. It's used for everything from round steak or quail to snap beans, corn, and okra. Smothering involves cooking ingredients very quickly in oil— sometimes after flouring them—over fairly high heat, then cooking them very slowly and for a long time over very low heat. This method brings out sweet, subtle flavors in a way unmatched by any other style of cooking. You end up with a nice, naturally thick gravy, and a succulent dish. The result isn't always picture-pretty, but what you taste will easily persuade you to adapt the technique to other styles of cooking as well. You'll find yourself keeping an eye out in the grocery store for new ingredients to take home and smother. I know it's become fashionable to cook vegetables only very briefly, but comparing plain old steamed or sautéed green beans to Cajun Smothered Snap Beans is like comparing kissing your sister to the real thing. After all, people didn't cook vegetables this way for three hundred years out of sheer perversity—there's something universally appealing about that taste.

Smoking

Smoking is one of the oldest cooking methods—it was one of the ways people preserved meats and fish before refrigeration and modern canning methods. In this country, the smoked hams produced in Virginia are one of our oldest and proudest products. In southwest Louisiana, the tradition of the *boucherie*—the slaughtering of a pig—was the occasion for a day of work and celebration, during which every part of the animal was utilized. Much of the meat was smoked—as sausages or hams, or as tasso (strips of pork marinated for several days in seasonings before smoke-curing, and cured with more spices than Virginia hams). Even the lower shank meat could be used for this, to make a staple used in seasoning beans, soups, gumbos, and the like.

These days Louisiana is rediscovering smoking along with rest of the nation. Now that we no longer need it for preserving meats, we're exploring the possibilities of the tremendous flavor it offers. In the process, we're beginning to apply the technique not just to inexpensive cuts of meat, but to all sorts of ingredients our grandparents never thought of smoking—whole tenderloins of beef, and high grades of fish, game, and poultry.

It may surprise you to learn that smoking is amazingly simple. And it doesn't have to be expensive, either. In fact, if you have a barbecue grill with a cover sitting in the backyard, you can make your own smoker in an afternoon for virtually nothing. Here's how:

You'll need a small galvanized pail or pan (no larger across than two feet) that will fit below the rack that sits on top of the grill. This will hold the wood. Punch three or four holes about an inch in diameter in the bottom of the pail or pan. (You can do this with a screwdriver.)

Now you need some wood. In southwest Louisiana we're blessed with abundant hardwoods, so on our smoker we use pecan and oak. Texans say mesquite's the best, but in North Carolina, they maintain it's hickory. I suggest that you use a hardwood that's readily available in your area. Don't spend a lot of money on wood—work with what you have. The wood has to fit inside the pail or pan, so cut it to size accordingly. I prefer freshly cut green wood, because the moisture still inside the wood gives you more smoke. If you can't get green wood, soak the cut wood in water overnight.

Remove the grill from the barbecue and set the pail or pan inside, to one side (if there is only one bottom vent, place it on that side). Put a single layer of charcoal inside the pail or pan and light it as you normally would. Once the coals have turned white, layer on the wood as tight as possible, with the smaller pieces on the bottom, getting progressively larger to the top. Depending on what you're smoking, you may or may not need the rack—put it on if you do. Close the top and seal all the vents well except the one near the pail—leave it open a crack. You may need to use paper to seal the vents. That's all there is to making a smoker.

Some things to remember when using your smoker: Remember to check it every so often to be sure the wood hasn't caught fire—

if it has, pour a little water onto the wood until the flames are extinguished. Also check whether you need more wood. Keep pressing the logs down so that the wood stays directly on top of the coals—sometimes a log gets hung up and doesn't fall. Another tip: Cut an old broom handle to exactly the width of your grill and cover it with aluminum foil. Use it as a rod for smoking turkeys, chicken, sausage, or even tasso. Wedged securely above the notches designed to hold the rack in place, the rod allows meats, etc., to hang freely with smoke circulating all around.

There's no set recipe for smoking chickens and turkeys, but here are a couple of good hints: Season the bird several hours ahead, or the night before, with plenty of salt and ground red, black, and white peppers. (I recommend that you try a chicken first to get the hang of it, before tackling a bigger bird.) Exactly how long it will take to smoke depends on several factors—how intense the heat is in the smoker, how tender the bird, etc. A fresh young fryer usually takes 2½–3 hours on my smoker. Once you feel comfortable with your smoker, let yourself go. Try smoking fresh sausage—it will take 4–6 hours. By now you should be comfortable enough with your smoker to know how often you'll need to check it. We use a simple converted-barbecue smoker at the restaurant, and we're so familiar with it that we can judge the intensity of the heat simply by putting our hands close to the outside lid—and whether it needs more wood by the amount of smoke that seeps out around the edges. The more you use your smoker, the easier it will become.

Are you ready for a turkey? Remember that it's a big bird and will take a lot longer. Like any poultry, a turkey should be smoked breast side down so that all the juices will flow there and it won't dry out. It'll be the best turkey you ever tasted. And there's no better gumbo than a Leftover Turkey and Sausage Gumbo. You can also take fresh hens and smoke them 5–6 hours—they won't be quite done—then boil them until tender, 2–3 hours. Debone them and use the meat and stock and smoked sausage (your own!) to make Chicken and Sausage Gumbo.

If you love fresh fish, as I hope you do, try smoking some. Place a single layer of nice firm fish directly on the grill. You can use whole fish or fillets, skinned or not. I prefer fillets because they allow you to get maximum smoke flavor into the fish quickly, before it dries out. Let the fish smoke for about 2 hours, then re-move—it won't be cooked all the way, but it will be nice and smoky. Place the fish in a shallow pan with the sauce for Shrimp Ms. Ann, a light lemon and butter sauce, and finish cooking under the broiler—it shouldn't take more than 2–3 minutes. This might sound like a big fuss over plain old broiled fish, but after you taste it, I guarantee you'll find a fancy name for it.

As you'll discover, smoking has really come a long way, from a simple food preservative to today's creative and varied technique—in effect, it's both a cooking process and a seasoning. But just because it's used for more doesn't mean it's harder—it's easy, and once you've tried it, you'll be as hooked as I am. Try applying it to some of the basic ingredients in a familiar recipe and see what a difference it makes. Pretty soon you'll be coming up with creations of your own.

Utensils

It used to be that when a young southwest Louisiana couple got married, some of the gifts they treasured were those intended for the kitchen. And the ones they treasured most were used black iron cookware. The young bride knew that those pots had been cherished by the housewife who parted with them, for the job of cooking was much easier without having to fool with unseasoned—and often poorer quality—pots and pans. These days we not only have gas and electric ranges whose heat we can easily control, but good, heavy-duty cookware made of everything from good old cast iron to heavy-gauge aluminum to lined copper and stainless steel. You don't need much cookware for Cajun cooking—virtually every recipe in this book can be made with a large heavy skillet, a Dutch oven or other large heavy pot, a couple of saucepans and mixing bowls, a stockpot, and a large shallow baking pan.

Hors d'Oeuvres
and Appetizers

Strictly speaking, fussy appetizers and fancy hors d'oeuvres don't have much to do with traditional Cajun food. This makes a lot of sense—when people don't have much money and do hard physical work all day, they like to sit down to hearty, main-course food that gets right to the point. What has always been a part of Cajun culture, though, is pulling out the stops—both in and out of the kitchen—for big celebrations. Weddings, holidays, after-funeral receptions, and casual as well as formal open houses on New Year's Day and similar occasions were especially precious when they provided a rare break from daily labor and an even rarer chance to get together with friends and relatives from beyond the household. And while modern transportation and communication have made staying in touch with family and friends a lot easier for Cajuns as well as for everybody else, those big celebrations—and the festive buffet tables around which they revolve—have remained an important part of Cajun life. Some of the dishes that grace those splendid buffet tables are very old, like Daube Glacé, a Cajun terrine. Others—Shrimp Mold, Hot Crab Dip—are typical ways of making a very little go a very long way even when you're really living it up. These dishes adapt wonderfully to cocktail parties and the like, and they also work beautifully as first courses at more formal sit-down dinners.

Of course, as Cajun food has gone public, Cajun chefs have made the most of changing circumstances, as always, and have developed dishes in their tradition that fit more standard notions of appetizers and first courses. Oysters Edele and my version of Shrimp Rémoulade are two popular dishes from the menu at Patout's that will start the fanciest company dinner off in style. And many main-course dishes, served in small portions, make perfect starters that really wake up your taste buds. In fact, the beginning of a meal is a good place to introduce Cajun into your cooking—whenever family and friends gather at the table, there's a touch of festivity, an openness, a desire for excitement. So start Cajun, and you'll find that the rest follows naturally.

☜ CHEESE BISCUITS ☞

6 ounces cream cheese, at room temperature
1 cup (¹/₂ pound) butter, at room temperature

¹/₂ teaspoon salt
2 cups all-purpose flour

Cream together the cream cheese and butter until light. Combine the salt and flour and stir in. Turn half the dough out onto a floured surface and roll out to a thickness of about ¼ inch. Cut into 1½- to 2-inch rounds. Then roll out and cut the rest of the dough. Place the rounds on a buttered cookie sheet and bake in a preheated 375°F oven for 10–12 minutes, or until browned. Serve hot.

Makes 1½–2 dozen.

❧ CHEESE STRAWS ❧

1 cup (¹/₂ pound) butter
3 cups all-purpose flour
2 teaspoons baking powder
2 teaspoons salt

2 teaspoons ground red
pepper
1 pound sharp Cheddar
cheese, grated

Cream the butter until soft and fluffy. Sift together the flour, baking powder, salt, and pepper and add to the butter along with the cheese. Knead these ingredients lightly with your fingers in the bowl until the mixture holds together.

Using a cookie press or a pastry bag, pipe strips about ¼ inch thick, 1½ inches wide, and 6 inches long onto a buttered cookie sheet (or you can pipe strips the length of the sheet and cut them at 6-inch intervals before or after baking).

Bake in a preheated 350°F oven for about 10 minutes, or just until golden (don't let them get too brown). Store in tightly covered tins when cool.

These will keep for several weeks.

Makes about 2 dozen.

❧ DAUBE GLACÉ ❧

This is a very old dish. It was traditionally served at Cajun weddings and receptions because it could make a little bit of roast go a long way—and it used every delicious drop of the pan juices.

1 round roast of veal or beef, about 4 pounds	2 medium bell peppers
1 pork roast, about 3 pounds	½ cup chopped green onions
6 garlic cloves, slivered	½ cup finely chopped parsley
Salt and pepper	4 quarts water
Tabasco sauce	4 large fresh pig's feet
¼ cup vegetable oil	2 pounds pork skins (or 4 additional pig's feet)
3 medium onions, chopped fine	1 envelope unflavored gelatin (optional)
4 celery stalks, chopped fine	

Cut slits at even intervals in the surface of the roasts and insert slivers of garlic. Sprinkle the meat with salt, pepper, and Tabasco sauce. Heat the oil in a Dutch oven or roasting pan over high heat, add the meat, and brown well on all sides. Cover and bake in a preheated 325°F oven for 2 hours. Chop the onions, celery, and bell peppers medium fine, sprinkle over the meat, cover again, and continue cooking in the oven for another 30 minutes. Remove the meat from the pot and let cool. Add the green onions and the parsley to the juices in the pan.

While the meat is cooking, boil the pig's feet and pork skins in the water for about an hour to make the gelatin. (If you are short on pig's feet or pork skins, you can add 1 envelope of unflavored gelatin to the hot liquid to be sure that there is enough gelatin to hold the mold together.) Let cool.

When the meat is cool, cut it into chunks about ½ inch thick and 1 inch wide by 2 inches long. Place the meat in molds (use a large pan, two 8-cup ring molds, or a variety of large and small molds), alternating layers of veal and pork. Pour over any juices from the roasting pan and add enough of the gelatin mixture to cover the meat entirely. Refrigerate until firm (overnight or longer). You can prepare the daube up to this point and store it in the refrigerator, well wrapped, for 2 or 3 days. You can also refrigerate or freeze any extra stock.

Unmold on greens and serve as an appetizer, with bread or crackers, mustard, and mayonnaise. Garnish colorfully with lemons, radishes, celery leaves, and so on.

Fills two 8-cup molds.

❧ CAJUN PÂTÉ ❧

This pâté is a bit different from most French pâtés—it's actually closer to Jewish chopped liver. We like to make it at Christmastime, pack it in crocks, and give it as gifts.

2 cups (1 pound) butter
2 or 3 shallots, minced
1/8 teaspoon dried thyme,
    or 1/2 teaspoon fresh
1 bay leaf, crushed

1/2 pound chicken livers
1 teaspoon Cognac
Salt and pepper
Tabasco sauce

Melt the butter over medium heat. Add the shallots, thyme, and bay leaf and cook until the shallots are soft, 2–3 minutes. Add the livers and cook for 3 minutes longer, stirring constantly. Transfer the mixture to a blender or a food processor fitted with a steel blade and puree until smooth. Blend in the Cognac and salt, pepper, and Tabasco sauce to taste.

Pour into a bowl and set aside to cool to room temperature. Beat thoroughly two or three times during the first hour to keep the ingredients from separating. Then refrigerate until cold. Pack into jars or crocks and chill again.

Serve cold, with Melba toast or crackers.

Makes about 2 cups.

❧ STUFFED MUSHROOMS ❧

This recipe is essentially an adaptation of the Cajun Crab Dressing we use in a number of main dishes. Paired with mushrooms, it makes a wonderful appetizer.

12 large mushrooms
1 medium onion
1 medium bell pepper
1 celery rib
1 cup (¹/₂ pound) butter
1 pound white crab meat
¹/₄ cup plus 3 tablespoons lemon juice
¹/₄ cup plus 2 tablespoons chopped green onions
¹/₄ cup plus 2 tablespoons chopped parsley

1 cup bread crumbs
1 tablespoon plus a dash of Worcestershire sauce
1 tablespoon plus a dash of Tabasco sauce
1 tablespoon salt
1¹/₂ teaspoons ground red pepper
1 teaspoon black pepper
1 teaspoon white pepper
2 tablespoons vermouth

Remove the stems from the mushrooms and reserve them for another use. Wipe the caps.

Chop the onion, bell pepper, and celery fine and sauté in ¹/₄ pound of the butter until soft. Stir in the crab meat and ¹/₄ cup of the lemon juice and simmer for 10 minutes. Add 2 tablespoons each of the green onions and parsley, all the bread crumbs, and a dash each of Worcestershire and Tabasco sauce. Simmer 4–5 minutes more, stirring often. Season with salt and pepper to taste. Remove dressing from heat and let cool.

Stuff the mushroom caps generously with the dressing and place in a single layer in a shallow ovenproof dish. Melt the remaining ¼ pound butter and add the remaining 3 tablespoons lemon juice and 1 tablespoon each of Worcestershire and Tabasco sauce, and the vermouth. Simmer together for 1 minute, pour over the mushrooms, and bake in a preheated 350°F oven for 15 minutes, or broil at 450°F for 5 minutes.

Serves 4 as a first course.

❦ OYSTERS EDELE ❦

A Cajun oyster stew—but not your typical cream-based New England stew. This one has a dark roux base that really comes through. Served in pastry, it's a show-stopping starter.

2 cups dark roux (see Basics)	1 teaspoon red pepper
4–6 cups oyster liquor	½ teaspoon black pepper
1 cup chopped green onions	½ teaspoon white pepper
1 cup chopped parsley	8–10 good shots Tabasco sauce
3 dozen shucked unwashed oysters	10 individual puff pastry shells,
2 teaspoons salt	prebaked

Warm the roux over low heat in a black iron skillet. Stir in as much of the oyster liquor as the roux will hold without becoming liquid—the mixture will become fluffy, like a mousse. Raise the heat to medium-high and add the green onions, parsley, oysters, and seasonings. Stir continuously, until the oysters curl around the edges. The mixture should be as thick as a chicken stew. If it is too thick, add a little more oyster liquor. Serve immediately in hot pastry shells.

Serves 10.

❦ MARINATED CRAB FINGERS ❧

A lot of people make the mistake of thinking that the body and claws of a crab are the only worthwhile eating parts. This dish— succulent crab fingers marinated in a tangy vinaigrette—proves how wrong they are. Prepared this way, the fingers make a delicious cocktail snack or first course. And they're fun to eat—sucking out the meat has a way of loosening up your guests. Most fish stores sell precooked crab fingers by the pound, which makes this recipe especially easy. You can also try it with the fingers left from a crab boil, or with crab or lobster claws, or even with the meat from Alaskan king crab legs.

1 pound boiled crab fingers
Juice of 2 lemons
1 tablespoon fresh basil, or
  1 teaspoon dried
2 teaspoons fresh thyme, or
  ¹/₂ teaspoon dried

¹/₂ cup olive oil
2 teaspoons red wine vinegar
1 teaspoon salt
1 teaspoon ground black
  pepper
1 tablespoon chopped parsley

Place the crab fingers in a large bowl. Mix together the remaining ingredients and pour over. Combine well, cover, and refrigerate several hours or overnight.

Serves 10–12 as an appetizer.

❧ HOT CRAB DIP ❧

A great basic hot dip that can be endlessly adapted. Try it with lobster or shrimp—either minced or, if they are tiny, left whole.

1/2 cup (1/4 pound) butter
2 medium yellow onions, chopped
  fine
1 small bell pepper, chopped
  fine
2 garlic cloves, minced
1 pint heavy cream
1 cup chopped green onions
1/2 cup chopped parsley

1 tablespoon fresh basil, or
  1 teaspoon dried
1 tablespoon fresh thyme, or
  1 teaspoon dried
2 teaspoons salt
2 teaspoons ground black pepper
1 teaspoon ground white pepper
5–6 shots Tabasco sauce
1 pound fresh white crab meat

Melt the butter in a medium saucepan over medium heat. Add the onions, bell pepper, and garlic and sauté for 10–15 minutes, until wilted. Stir in the cream and bring to a simmer. Stir in the green onions, parsley, herbs, and seasonings and continue to simmer until the cream has reduced by about a quarter and the sauce is thick. Stir in the crab meat, return to a simmer, and let cook 2–3 minutes more. Pour into a chafing dish and serve as an hors d'oeuvre or as part of a buffet with crackers or Melba toast (I especially like it with garlic Melba toast).

Makes about 1 quart.

❧ SEAFOOD MOLD ☙

This is a very elegant, very easy dish, a good way to use leftovers you may have on hand, or at least to let you indulge in seafood without breaking your budget. Because it must also be prepared in advance, it's an ideal party dish.

2 envelopes unflavored gelatin
1 cup seafood stock (see Basics)
2 cups cooked, chopped seafood
  (shrimp, crawfish, crab)
1 cup finely chopped celery
1/3 cup finely chopped parsley
1/3 cup finely chopped green onion
2 tablespoons lemon juice
Couple dashes of Tabasco sauce

Couple dashes of Worcestershire
  sauce
1 tablespoon minced fresh basil
  (optional)
2 teaspoons minced fresh thyme
  (optional)
Salt and pepper to taste
8 ounces cream cheese
1 cup mayonnaise (see page 156)

Let the gelatin soften in the seafood stock in a small saucepan.

Mix together the seafood, celery, parsley, green onion, lemon juice, Tabasco and Worcestershire sauces, optional fresh herbs, and salt and pepper to taste. In a separate bowl, cream together the cream cheese and mayonnaise. Stir in the seafood mixture and blend well.

Place the gelatin mixture over low heat and stir just until the gelatin dissolves. Stir into the seafood mixture and blend well. Pour into a 5-cup mold or several smaller molds. Chill until firm, several hours or overnight. Unmold and garnish as desired. Serve with toast triangles or crackers.

This keeps well in the refrigerator for 2 or 3 days.

Serves 10–12 as a first course, more as part of a buffet.

❧ SHRIMP RÉMOULADE ❧

This recipe makes about a quart of rémoulade sauce—more than you will need for this quantity of shrimp, but it does not work well in smaller quantities. The extra will keep well in the refrigerator for 2 to 3 weeks.

1 pound medium shrimp,	*¹/₂ teaspoon ground red pepper*
heads off	*¹/₂ teaspoon ground white pepper*
1 quart water	*¹/₂ teaspoon ground black pepper*
2 tablespoons salt	

Peel and devein the shrimp. Bring the water, salt, and peppers to a full boil in a medium saucepan over high heat. Drop in the shrimp and stir. Continue to cook over high heat for 4–5 minutes, stirring often, until the shrimp are pink and firm. (Shrimp will cook at 160°F, so start timing as soon as you add them.) Do not bring back to a boil. Drain the shrimp and cool them quickly in the refrigerator or by placing ice on them.

Rémoulade Sauce

1 cup olive oil	*1¹/₂ teaspoons salt*
1 cup vinegar	*¹/₂ cup white horseradish*
1¹/₃ cups Creole or Dijon	*¹/₄ cup mayonnaise (see page 156)*
mustard	*3 cups minced celery*
¹/₃ cup paprika	*²/₃ cup minced parsley*
1 tablespoon ground black pepper	*¹/₃ cup minced onion*

In a large mixing bowl, combine the olive oil, vinegar, mustard, paprika, pepper, salt, horseradish, and mayonnaise. Add the celery, parsley, and onion and mix well.

When you are ready to serve, place the shrimp in a mixing bowl, add a generous amount of the rémoulade sauce (2–3 cups) and mix well. Serve on a bed of lettuce as an appetizer or first course.

Serves 6–8.

❧ SHRIMP CROQUETTES ❧

Again, in true Cajun fashion, this recipe can be modified to make use of a variety of seafood—use what's freshest. I love it with crawfish, and crab or lobster—or any combination.

2 pounds small fresh shrimp, heads off	2 teaspoons salt
¼ pound (½ cup) butter	1 teaspoon ground red pepper
2 medium yellow onions, chopped fine	1 teaspoon ground black pepper
1 small bell pepper, chopped fine	½ teaspoon ground white pepper
3 garlic cloves, minced	1 cup chopped green onions
	½ cup finely chopped parsley
	½ cup fresh bread crumbs

Peel and devein the shrimp; roughly chop them and reserve. Melt the butter in a medium saucepan and add the onions, bell pepper, and garlic. Sauté over medium heat 20–25 minutes, until very soft. Stir in the salt and peppers and the chopped shrimp and sauté just until the shrimp turn pink, 5–7 minutes. Remove from heat and stir in the green onions, parsley, and bread crumbs. Transfer the mixture to a large shallow pan and place in the refrigerator for at least 2 hours, to chill it quickly. This is your shrimp dressing; you can prepare it in advance to this point and store it in the refrigerator for a day or two.

Croquettes

1 tablespoon salt	*2 cups milk*
2 teaspoons ground red pepper	*3 eggs*
1 teaspoon ground black pepper	*3 cups corn flour*
1 teaspoon ground white pepper	*Vegetable oil for deep-frying*

In a small bowl, mix together the salt and peppers; set aside. Beat together the milk, eggs, and half the salt-pepper mixture in a medium bowl. Combine the corn flour with the rest of the salt-pepper mixture and place in a large shallow pan. Pour vegetable oil into a deep-fryer or other large heavy pot to a depth of about 3 inches and heat to 350°F.

Remove the shrimp dressing from the refrigerator and shape into balls about 1 inch in diameter. (If the mixture seems too loose, stir in additional bread crumbs until it holds together.) Dip the balls in the batter, then roll them in the corn flour mixture. Transfer them to the hot oil and fry until golden brown, 3–4 minutes. Don't crowd the pot—you'll probably need to fry them in two batches. Drain on paper toweling and serve as an hors d'oeuvre or appetizer, with cocktail sauce or homemade Tartar Sauce (see page 90).

Serves 6–8.

❧ STUFFED ARTICHOKES ❧

Strictly speaking, this recipe isn't Cajun, except that, in true Cajun fashion, it lets you take advantage of artichokes when they're plentiful and cheap. You can make a large batch then, and freeze the extra for when they're no longer in season.

6 good-size artichokes
1½ pounds bacon, sliced
10 cups Italian-style bread
   crumbs
1½ cups grated Romano cheese
1½ cups grated Parmesan cheese
1 cup chopped green onions

½ cup chopped parsley
6–10 garlic cloves, chopped fine
2 tablespoons salt
1 tablespoon ground red pepper
1 tablespoon ground black pepper
2½–3 cups olive oil
6 slices lemon

Slice off the pointed leaf ends of the artichokes. Slice off the stem ends so that they will sit up straight.

Fry the bacon until very crisp, drain thoroughly, and crumble fine by hand into a bowl. Mix in the bread crumbs, cheeses, green onions, parsley, garlic, salt, and peppers.

Spread the leaves of each artichoke as much as possible and pack in a generous amount of stuffing around them. Tap the artichokes lightly to let any loose stuffing fall off. Stand them in a casserole or roasting pan just large enough to hold them in a single layer. Add water to a depth of 1½ inches. Pour a generous amount of olive oil over each artichoke, letting it seep in. Top each with a slice of lemon. Bring the water to a boil, cover, lower heat, and steam the artichokes until the leaves pull out easily, 1 hour or more. Check the water level after about 25 minutes and add more if needed.

Serve hot or warm.

You can prepare the artichokes ahead and reheat before serving. Leftover stuffing will keep in the refrigerator for a couple of weeks and longer in the freezer.

Serves 6.

Gumbos
and Soups

As with appetizers, gumbos and soups don't fit into traditional Cajun cooking quite the way, say, consommé fits into classic
French cooking. But in this respect they're true to the origins of
soup the world over—they're flavorful, satisfying dishes, more stews
than soups, sturdy enough to sustain a meal by themselves.

Probably no other dish reflects the essence of Cajun food as well
as gumbo, which is the very embodiment of using precious little
to serve a great many, and to serve them well. It's more accurate,
though, to think of gumbo as a category of dishes, or a technique,
than as one specific dish. Gumbos tend to look alike, but no two
taste alike—each is so unique that you could fix one a week and
not get tired of gumbo all year long, or even feel that you were
eating the same way all the time. One of the greatest misconcep-
tions about gumbo is that it has to do only with okra or filé. An
African word for okra is *gumbo,* which helps explain part of this
misunderstanding, and in many of my gumbos I do use okra—I'll
explain how to prepare it for freezing when it's in season, too, so
that you can try using it in combination with other gumbo ingredients as they come into season. I don't use filé at all—it thickens
the broth, but it adds no flavor, and in Cajun cooking that's cheat-
ing. You'll find that once you've mastered a few basic recipes—
Shrimp and Okra or Chicken and Sausage, which are good ones to

start with—making gumbo is the perfect way to appreciate what's best and freshest in your neck of the woods at any given time of year.

In my home, we still make a meal of gumbo, which we always serve with a bowl of potato salad alongside. But again, as Cajun food has entered restaurants, cooks and customers have discovered that it makes a wonderful first course. Other soups, too, lend themselves to this treatment—delicate Oyster and Artichoke Soup, and Corn and Crab Bisque, which raises the Cajun habit of never throwing anything away to an art.

And then there is a class of dishes too glorious and complex in flavor to be called mere soups, delicacies that rank with the great French bouillabaisse: Shrimp and Crab Stew, a little thicker than a gumbo; Crawfish Bisque, similar in consistency to a gumbo but elevated to another realm by the addition of savory stuffed crawfish heads; Turtle Soup, an old and honorable way to handle other kinds of game as well, or the tougher cuts of meat; and the classic Redfish Courtbouillon for which Louisiana is justly famous.

But don't waste time envying us Cajuns the amazing variety of available ingredients that gave birth to the infinite variety of soups, gumbos, bisques, and stews we enjoy. Get started cooking—and while your stock simmers, think about how to match the techniques you're learning with the special delicacies *your* region boasts. I've always wanted, for example, to try our Crawfish Bisque with a nice fresh lobster. Maybe you'll beat me to it.

❧ CHICKEN AND OKRA GUMBO ❧

It's easy to enjoy okra-based gumbos year-round, even though you can get okra only in the summertime. Just slice it and smother it down with the vegetables and chicken stock as directed, let it cool, and freeze it in plastic. When you see shrimp or chicken on special in May, or get a hankering for a nice hot bowl of gumbo in January, just thaw the okra and proceed with the recipe.

2 young chickens,
   2½–3 pounds each
2 tablespoons salt
2 teaspoons ground red pepper
2 teaspoons ground black pepper
1 teaspoon ground white pepper
2 pounds tender okra,
   thin sliced
2 large onions, chopped coarse

3 large tomatoes, peeled and
   chopped coarse
1 medium bell pepper, chopped
   coarse
3 cups chicken stock (1 quart)
   (see Basics)
½ cup chopped green onions
½ cup chopped parsley
2 tablespoons of dark roux

Cut the chicken into serving pieces, setting aside the fat from the neck and back cavities. Sprinkle with half the salt and peppers. Render the reserved fat in a Dutch oven or other heavy pot (if your pot is not well seasoned, you may have to add a little oil). Add the chicken and brown on all sides over medium-high heat. Remove the chicken to a platter.

Add the okra, onions, tomatoes, and bell pepper to the pan and season with salt and peppers. Add the chicken stock, cover, and cook over medium heat, stirring often, until okra is tender, 45 minutes to 1 hour. Uncover and add the roux. Cook another 30 minutes. Then add the chicken and the remaining salt and peppers, and continue to cook, stirring often, until the chicken is tender, 45 minutes to 1 hour more. Stir in the green onions and parsley and simmer 5 minutes longer.

Serve in bowls, over rice (or serve the rice alongside).

Serves 6–8.

❧ SEAFOOD GUMBO ❧

This is a classic gumbo, and very likely one of the first you'll think of trying. Don't be put off by the length of the recipe—it's really just a series of simple steps, and you can shorten the process considerably by preparing okra in advance when it's in season, as described above.

2 tablespoons salt
2 teaspoons ground red pepper
2 teaspoons ground black pepper
1 teaspoon ground white pepper
1 pound fresh okra, sliced ¼ inch
    thick
½ cup vegetable oil
1 teaspoon white vinegar
2 cups water
3 large tomatoes, peeled and
    roughly chopped

4 medium onions,
    chopped fine
6 fresh crabs (I use blue crabs)
2 pounds medium fresh
    shrimp, heads off
3 medium bell peppers,
    chopped fine
1½ cups dark roux
    (see Basics)
1 cup chopped green onions
1 cup finely chopped parsley

In a small bowl, mix together the salt and peppers; set aside.

Place the okra, oil, vinegar, water, tomatoes, one quarter of the onions, and 2 teaspoons of the salt-pepper mixture in a large (8–10-quart) heavy pot. Mix well, place over medium heat, and cover. Cook 45 minutes to 1 hour, stirring often. If the mixture begins to stick, just stir it, scraping the bottom of the pot well. (You can add a little water if it makes you feel better.)

While the okra is cooking, half fill a large stockpot with water and bring to a boil. Add the crabs, cover, and cook for 4 minutes. Drain the crabs and let cool. Peel and devein the shrimp, and place the peels in the empty stockpot. When the crabs have cooled enough to handle, detach the claws, crack both joints, and add them to the stockpot. Remove the crab fingers and add them, too. Add 6 quarts of water, bring to a boil, and let boil slowly for 1 hour. Remove the stock from the heat, strain it, return it to the pot, and place over medium heat. Discard the shrimp heads and peels; you can reserve the crab claws and fingers for the finished gumbo if you like. Add the remaining onions, the bell peppers, the cooked okra, the remaining salt-pepper mixture, and the roux. Stir well, bring to a boil, and let simmer for 1–1½ hours. The gumbo should not be too thick—it should run freely off a spoon. (If it becomes too thick, add water.)

While the gumbo is cooking, back to the crabs. Scrape any crab fat from the sides of the shells into a bowl and discard the shells (or save them for Crab Eugene, page 70). Remove the gills from each side of the crabs and discard. Spoon out the rest of the crab fat and organs from the body cavity and add it to the bowl of crab fat. Break the crab bodies in half and slice them horizontally to expose the meat. Mash the crab fat and organs or puree them briefly in a food processor. Add to the gumbo as it cooks.

Add the crab bodies to the gumbo and continue to simmer over low heat for 45 minutes to 1 hour. At this point you can stop. If you are cooking your gumbo for the next day (Cajun folks know that a gumbo tastes better the second and third day), remove from the heat and let cool. If you like, you can remove the crabs from the gumbo, pick out the meat, and return it to the pot, discarding the shells. (For a casual meal, leaving the meat in the shells is fine, and you can also add in the claws and fingers from the stock.) When you are ready to serve, bring the gumbo to a slow simmer over medium heat. Add the shrimp and let cook until they are pink and firm, 4–6 minutes. Stir in the green onions and parsley, remove from the heat, and serve in large soup bowls over beds of cooked rice.

Serves 6–8.

❧ SHRIMP AND OKRA GUMBO ❧

If you can possibly get your hands on fresh shrimp with their heads still on, use them here (just increase the poundage). The shrimp flavor you'll get from using the heads in your stock will come right through the okra and will make a big difference for the final dish.

2–3 pounds medium fresh shrimp, heads off
3 quarts water
1/2 cup vegetable oil
5 pounds fresh okra, sliced thin
3 medium onions, chopped fine
3 medium bell peppers, sliced thin
2 celery ribs, sliced thin
6–8 medium ripe tomatoes, peeled and coarsely chopped (if good tomatoes are not available, substitute two 15-ounce cans whole peeled tomatoes)

1 teaspoon white vinegar
1 teaspoon ground red pepper
1 teaspoon ground black pepper
1 teaspoon ground white pepper
4–5 good shots Tabasco sauce
Salt
1/2 cup chopped green onions
1/2 cup chopped parsley
2 tablespoons dark roux

Remove the heads from the shrimp (if they're not already headless) and peel and devein them. Place the heads and peelings in a 4–6-quart stockpot and add the water. Bring to a boil, reduce heat, and boil slowly for 45 minutes to 1 hour, to reduce by half. Strain.

Heat the oil in another large heavy pot (6–8-quart) and add the okra, onions, bell peppers, celery, tomatoes, vinegar, half the stock, the peppers, Tabasco sauce, and salt to taste. Cover and bring to a simmer over medium-high heat. Reduce the heat and continue to simmer, covered, stirring often, until the okra is very tender, an hour or more. If the mixture starts to dry out, add additional stock. Add the rest of the stock and roux and continue cooking uncovered for another 30 to 45 minutes. (You can prepare this much ahead.)

Add the shrimp to the hot okra mixture and cook over medium-high heat until the shrimp turn pink, about 5 minutes. Add a little more stock if the gumbo seems too thick. Stir in the green onions and parsley.

Serve in additional bowls over rice (or serve the rice alongside).

Serves 8–10.

Note: If you have some leftover crab meat, add it to the gumbo with the shrimp.

CHICKEN AND SAUSAGE GUMBO

There's no excuse for not making this gumbo—you can get the basic ingredients just about anywhere. Along with Seafood Gumbo, Chicken Gumbo is considered classic, and the addition of a smoky sausage gives this one a nice balance of flavors.

1 tablespoon salt
1½ teaspoons ground red pepper
1 teaspoon ground black pepper
1 teaspoon ground white pepper
1 roasting chicken or hen, 3–5 pounds
2 cups medium roux (see Basics)
2 large onions, chopped fine
2 bell peppers, chopped fine

3 celery ribs, chopped fine
1 gallon chicken stock (see Basics)
2 pounds smoked pork sausage, sliced ½ inch thick
1 cup chopped green onions
1 cup chopped parsley
4–6 shakes Tabasco sauce

In a small bowl, mix together the salt and peppers; set aside. Pull off the fat from the chicken neck and back cavities and set aside; cut the chicken into small serving pieces. Sprinkle half of the salt-pepper mixture over the chicken pieces. In a large heavy skillet, render the reserved chicken neck and back fat. Add the chicken pieces, brown on all sides, and remove. If you have not made your roux in advance, make it in the skillet, scraping loose any particles from the bottom and using the fat in the pan as part of the oil. If your roux is already made, add it to the skillet and get it good and hot. Add half the onions, bell peppers, and celery, stir well, and set aside to cook, stirring occasionally.

Place the stock and the remaining onions, bell peppers, and celery in a large (6–8-quart) heavy pot and bring to a boil. Gradually stir in the roux. Add the rest of the salt-pepper mixture and let simmer for 45 minutes to 1 hour. Add the chicken and sausage and continue to simmer slowly for at least 1½ hours, or until the chicken is tender. (The older the bird, the longer it takes.) If the gumbo becomes too thick, add water. Remove from the heat and let sit 15 minutes. Skim off the fat and discard. Stir in the green onions, parsley, and tabasco and let sit a few minutes more. Serve in large bowls over rice.

Serves 6–8.

❧ CHICKEN AND OYSTER GUMBO ❧

*1 hen, 3–4 pounds, fresh if
   possible*
2 cups dark roux (see Basics)
2 medium onions, chopped coarse
2 bell peppers, chopped coarse
2 celery ribs, chopped coarse
2 quarts chicken stock (see Basics)
3 cups oyster liquor (optional)

1 tablespoon salt
2 teaspoons ground red pepper
1 teaspoon ground white pepper
1½ teaspoons ground black pepper
1 cup chopped green onions
1 cup chopped parsley
*2 dozen unwashed shucked
   oysters*

Cut the hen into small serving pieces (halve the thighs and cut the breasts in thirds), reserving the fat from the neck and back cavities. Rub half the seasonings on the chicken. Render the fat in a Dutch oven or other heavy pot over medium-high heat (if your pot is not well seasoned you may need to add a little oil). Add the chicken pieces and brown on all sides. Remove the chicken to a platter.

(If you have not made the roux in advance, make it in the pot at this point, adding oil to the chicken fat to give you the necessary amount. Proceed according to the instructions for making roux under Basics.)

Warm the roux over low heat. Add the onions, bell peppers, celery, stock, and 2½ cups of the oyster liquor. (If you can't get oyster liquor, mix the oysters with 3 cups water and a little salt and let stand for 30 minutes. Strain and use the oyster water in place of the oyster liquor.) Add the other half of the seasoning mix. Bring to the boil, reduce heat, and simmer, stirring often, for 1 hour or more.

Add the chicken and continue to simmer for 1–2 hours, or until chicken is tender (remember, it takes a while for a hen to cook). Remove from heat and let stand 10–15 minutes. Skim fat, then stir in the green onions and parsley. Let stand a couple of minutes more. Bring the oysters and the remaining ½ cup oyster liquor (or oyster water) to a boil over high heat in a small saucepan. As soon as the oysters curl around the edges, remove from the heat.

Spoon a little rice into individual bowls, top each serving with 4 oysters, and ladle the gumbo over.

Serves 6.

❧ LEFTOVER TURKEY AND SAUSAGE GUMBO ❧

The universal question asked in all American households on the Friday morning after Thanksgiving is "What the hell am I gonna do with all this turkey?" In the true Cajun tradition of never throwing anything away, this gumbo gives you the answer—and not just in November, but anytime you have a large leftover bird.

1 leftover turkey or other
   large bird (smoked is
   wonderful)
2–3 celery ribs, chopped
2 large yellow onions, chopped
2 medium bell peppers, chopped
2–3 cups medium roux (see
   Basics)

1 tablespoon salt
2 teaspoons ground red pepper
1 tablespoon ground black pepper
1 tablespoon ground white pepper
2 pounds smoked pork sausage,
   sliced ½ inch thick
2 cups chopped green onions
1 cup chopped parsley

Pull as much meat off the turkey as you can. Place the carcass in a large stockpot and add water to cover. Bring to a boil over high heat, reduce heat to medium, and let simmer 1–1½ hours. Remove the carcass and discard. Add the celery, onions, and bell peppers and gradually stir in enough roux to make a medium-heavy gumbo (it should drip from a spoon without clinging). Stir in the salt, peppers, and sausage and let simmer for another hour. Add the turkey meat and let cook 15–20 minutes more. Remove from the heat, stir in the green onions and parsley, and serve in large bowls over rice.

Serves 6–8.

❧ DUCK AND SAUSAGE GUMBO ❧

This gumbo is designed to make the most of the strong flavors of a game bird. You don't have to restrict yourself to wild duck—any other wildfowl or domestic duck will work as well. Whatever bird you use, together with the dark roux, the sausage, and the strong seasonings, it will make a gumbo whose flavors will really jump in your mouth.

3 tablespoons salt
1 tablespoon ground red pepper
1 tablespoon ground black pepper
2 teaspoons ground white pepper
2 ducks, 3–4 pounds each, cut into serving pieces
1 cup flour
1 cup oil
2–3 cups dark roux (see Basics)

6 quarts duck or chicken stock or water (see Basics)
2 large onions, chopped fine
2 bell peppers, chopped fine
2 celery ribs, chopped fine
1 pound andouille or other smoked sausage, sliced ¹/₂ inch thick
1 cup chopped green onions
1 cup finely chopped parsley

In a small bowl, mix together the salt and peppers; set aside. Place the duck pieces in a large bowl, add a third of the salt-pepper mixture, and rub it in well. Place the flour in a large flat pan, add 2 teaspoons of the salt-pepper mixture, and mix well. Add the duck pieces and dredge them well on all sides. Place the oil in a large heavy skillet over high heat. When it is very hot, add the duck pieces and brown very well and very quickly on all sides. Remove them from the pan and set aside.

(If you have not prepared the roux in advance, make it now, using the oil and drippings in the skillet as part of the oil.)

Place the stock in a large stockpot and add the onions, bell peppers, celery, the rest of the salt and pepper, and the roux. Bring to a boil over medium-high heat, reduce heat, and let simmer for 1 hour. Add the duck and sausage and let simmer until the duck is very tender (a domestic duck will take about 1 hour, a wild duck may take twice as long). If the gumbo becomes too thick, add a little water (it should run freely off a spoon). Remove the gumbo from the heat and let it sit for 10–15 minutes, to allow the fat to rise. Skim off the grease and discard. (You can prepare the gumbo this far in advance. Bring it back to a simmer before proceeding.) Stir in the green onions and parsley and let sit for 2 minutes more. Serve in large bowls over rice.

Serves 8–10.

DUCK WITH OYSTERS GUMBO

Prepare as above, but omit the sausage. After you have skimmed the fat from the finished gumbo, add 2 dozen fresh shucked oysters and cook 3–4 minutes more, or until the oysters curl around the edges. Finish as above.

❦ REDFISH COURTBOUILLON ❦

This recipe is more a technique than just a way of fixing redfish. It works well with almost any firm-fleshed fish. In fact, in the 1986 Seafood Superbowl in Tallahassee, Florida, one of the dishes that won us the Gold Cup was Mullet Courtbouillon.

4 cups medium-dark roux (see Basics)
1 can (15 ounce) tomato sauce
3 cups peeled, roughly chopped fresh tomatoes (5–6 large)
1 redfish, 6–10 pounds
8 quarts water
3 large carrots
3 celery ribs
3 onions, chopped coarse

3 bell peppers, chopped coarse
1 rib celery, chopped coarse
1 tablespoon salt
2 teaspoons ground black pepper
1½ teaspoons ground white pepper
2 teaspoons ground red pepper
4–6 shots Tabasco sauce
1 cup chopped green onions
1 cup chopped parsley
½ cup chopped hard-boiled eggs (optional)

Warm the roux in a well-seasoned skillet, as large and heavy as you have (black iron is best). Raise the heat and add the tomato sauce and tomatoes, stirring to mix thoroughly. Cook over medium-high heat, stirring frequently, until the oil begins to separate out around the edges (the roux will be a dark mahogany color). Remove from the heat and let cool.

Fillet the fish. Cut the bones in 3-inch sections and place with the head in a large (10-quart) stockpot. Add the water, carrots, and the 3 celery ribs and bring to a boil. Let boil slowly, uncovered, for 1–1½ hours. The stock should reduce to about 6 quarts. Strain well and return to the pot.

Skim off the fat that has separated from the roux and discard. Place the stock over medium-high heat and add the chopped onions, bell peppers, and celery. When it boils, gradually stir in enough roux to reach a consistency halfway between a stew and a gumbo (it should fall from a spoon in full, heavy drops). Add the salt and peppers and Tabasco. Reduce heat and let boil slowly for 45 minutes to 1 hour, stirring occasionally. Cut the fish into serving pieces and add to the courtbouillon. Cook 5–10 minutes more. Remove from the heat and let stand 5 minutes more. Skim off any grease from the surface and discard.

Stir in the green onions and parsley and serve immediately over rice in individual bowls. Garnish with chopped hard-boiled eggs, if desired.

Serves 8–10 as a first course, 6 as a main course.

Note: This dish depends on a good strong fish stock, which you can make ahead of time (see Basics) when you have a lot of fish and freeze for use in this dish. But a stock made from one fish will suffice.

❦ SHRIMP AND CRAB STEW ❧

This should really be called Cajun Riviera Stew. Growing up, we used to go down to our "camp" at Cypremort Point. While the kids went trolling for shrimp and crabs with Papa Gene, Mama would stay back at the camp preparing the roux. The best part of the day wasn't trolling—it was eating the stew.

3 cans (10 ounce) whole peeled tomatoes or 4 cups fresh tomatoes, peeled and chopped
5 cups medium-colored roux (see Basics)
5 medium onions
3 medium bell peppers
3 celery ribs
5 pounds medium raw shrimp in shells, heads on (or 3 pounds, heads off)

1 dozen live blue or other medium crabs
1 tablespoon salt
1½ teaspoons ground black pepper
1 teaspoon ground white pepper
2 teaspoons ground red pepper
4–6 shots Tabasco sauce
1 cup chopped green onions
1 cup chopped parsley

For this recipe I like to use Ro-tel tomatoes, because of the peppers that they have mixed in. Drain the tomatoes and put them in a bowl. Break them up with your fingers. Heat the roux over medium-high heat, add the tomatoes, and cook until the mixture is mahogany-colored, stirring often. Coarsely chop the onions, bell peppers, and celery, add them to the roux, remove from the heat, and let sit until the vegetables are soft and the roux is cool enough to touch, stirring occasionally (this will take a good half hour).

While the roux is cooling, remove the heads from the shrimp and peel them. Remove the claws from the crabs. Put the crab claws and shrimp heads and peels in a 10-quart stockpot and add 6 quarts water. Bring to a boil and boil slowly, uncovered, over medium-high heat for 45 minutes. Strain the stock, return to the pot, and set aside.

Heat a large kettle of water to boiling, add the crabs, return to the boil, and cook exactly 1 minute. Drain and let cool. Clean the crabs (see page 59) and cut them in half lengthwise, then again horizontally (with your knife parallel to the back) to expose the meat.

Bring the stock to a boil over medium heat, then add enough roux to make a thick sauce, a little at a time, stirring frequently (the sauce should drop from a spoon in thick beads). Add the salt, peppers, and Tabasco sauce. Let simmer for an hour or more, stirring occasionally. Add the quartered crabs and cook for another 45 minutes, then add the shrimp and cook for 10 minutes. Add the green onions and parsley and simmer 5 minutes more.

Serve in bowls. Don't forget the French bread!

Serves 8–10.

☙ CORN AND CRAB BISQUE ☙

When we say we put everything to good use, we mean it. If you're in the habit of throwing away corn cobs, this recipe will teach you to mend your ways—they make the wonderful stock that is the base for this delicate soup. In fact, if you make Macque Choux (page 146), save the cobs—you can use them in this recipe with the addition of a few extra ears of corn.

10 ears of corn, shucked and
    cleaned
2 tabblespoons butter
2 tablespoons all-purpose flour
1 quart heavy cream
Salt
1 teaspoon ground red pepper
1/2 teaspoon ground black pepper

1/2 teaspoon ground white pepper
2 teaspoons dried thyme, or
    1 tablespoon fresh
2 teaspoons dried basil, or 1
    tablespoon fresh
1 pound cooked white crab meat
1/2 cup chopped green onions
1/4 cup chopped parsley

Cut the kernels from the cobs; scrape the milk from the cobs and reserve (see page 146 for technique). Place the cobs in a 6-quart pot and add 4 quarts water. Bring to a boil, reduce heat to medium, and boil slowly for 45 minutes to 1 hour to reduce by half. Remove the cobs but do not strain.

Melt the butter in a large heavy saucepan over medium heat. Whisk in the flour, stirring continuously, to make a light roux. Cook the roux for 3–4 minutes, continuing to stir. Test the roux by cooking a little bit and tasting; when the raw taste of the flour is completely gone, the roux is done. It should be no darker than the color of rich cream.

Heat the cream and add it to the corn stock. Bring to a simmer over medium-high heat and whisk in the roux. Add the corn, the corn milk, the seasonings and herbs, and simmer 20–25 minutes. Stir in the crab meat and simmer 3–4 minutes more. Stir in the green onions and parsley and serve.

Serves 6–8.

❦ OYSTER AND ARTICHOKE SOUP ❧

This recipe is designed to show off two wonderful ingredients—fresh oysters and fresh artichokes. You can, however, substitute canned or frozen artichokes if fresh ones are unavailable, though the result won't be quite as good.

4 large fresh artichokes	1/2 teaspoon salt
1 quart water	1/4 teaspoon ground black pepper
1 quart heavy cream	1/4 teaspoon ground red pepper
1 pint oyster liquor or oyster water (see page 41)	1/4 teaspoon ground white pepper
1 teaspoon dried thyme, or 1 tablespoon fresh	2 dozen fresh oysters, shucked
	1/2 cup chopped parsley
1 teaspoon dried basil, or 1 tablespoon fresh	1/2 cup chopped green onions

Place the artichokes in a medium saucepan, add the water, and bring to a boil over medium-high heat. Reduce the heat, cover, and cook until the artichokes are tender. Remove the artichokes and let cool.

Pour the cooking liquid from the artichokes into a 4–6-quart stockpot, add the cream and oyster liquor, and bring to a boil over medium-high heat. Add the herbs, salt, and peppers and let simmer slowly, stirring often with a whisk to keep the soup smooth and the cream from curdling, about 30 minutes.

Meanwhile, separate the artichoke leaves and scoop their flesh into a small bowl, using a teaspoon. Cut the hearts into small pieces. Add the artichokes to the soup and continue to simmer for 20 minutes.

Just before serving, add the oysters, parsley, and green onions to the soup and let simmer just until the edges of the oysters curl, 4–5 minutes. Serve immediately.

Serves 6–8.

❧ TURTLE SOUP ❧

This soup is served in some of the finest households along St. Charles Avenue in New Orleans, and in some of the lowliest shacks along the levees. And the simple reason why is its terrific flavor. You'll also notice that the technique is a bit different from that of the other recipes in this chapter. Try using it with other ingredients—it works beautifully with squirrel, rabbit, alligator, or just plain beef. Don't assume that you can't get turtle meat, though—it can be ordered from suppliers who will ship it around the nation. Check with your fish store, or consult the list of Sources at the back of the book.

4–5 pounds turtle or beef bones	2 medium bell peppers, chopped fine
2–3 pounds cleaned turtle meat	2 celery ribs, chopped fine
1½ tablespoons salt	2 garlic cloves, minced
2 teaspoons ground red pepper	1 can (15 ounce) tomato sauce
2 teaspoons ground black pepper	1 tablespoon Worcestershire sauce
1 teaspoon ground white pepper	6 shots Tabasco sauce
1 cup all-purpose flour	6 hard-boiled eggs
¾ cup vegetable oil	1 cup chopped green onions
1 cup medium roux (see Basics)	1 cup chopped parsley
2 medium onions, chopped fine	½ cup dry sherry

Place the turtle bones in an 8–10-quart stockpot, add 6 quarts of water, and bring to a boil over medium-high heat. Let boil 1 hour. Discard the bones and skim the stock.

Meanwhile, cut the turtle meat into pieces about 1 by 2 inches. In a small bowl, mix together the salt and peppers and sprinkle a third of the mixture over the turtle meat. Mix the flour with another 2 teaspoons of the salt-pepper mixture, place it in a shallow pan, and roll the seasoned turtle meat in it to dredge lightly on all sides. Heat the oil in a Dutch oven or other large heavy pot over medium-high heat, add the turtle meat, and brown well on all sides. Remove to a platter.

If you have not made your roux in advance, make it now in the pot. If it is already made, pour it into the pot and get it good and hot. Add the onions, bell peppers, celery, and garlic to the hot roux and let cook over medium heat 10–15 minutes. Stir in the tomato sauce and simmer 5–10 minutes more. Stir in the turtle stock, bring to a boil, and add the rest of the salt-pepper mixture, the turtle meat, and the Worcestershire and Tabasco sauces. Let the soup simmer slowly until the meat is very tender, 1½–2 hours. If it gets too thick, stir in a little water.

Just before serving, separate the yolks and whites of the hard-boiled eggs. Chop the whites and reserve. Mash the yolks with a little of the soup stock and stir them back into the soup. Stir in the chopped green onions and parsley, remove from heat, and let stand 5–10 minutes. Serve in gumbo or large soup bowls, garnishing each with a little of the chopped egg whites and a tablespoonful of sherry.

Serves 6–8.

Seafood

When Louisianians think of seafood, we think first of crawfish—one of the best products nature has to offer, as the rest of the country is discovering. Louisiana is blessed in other ways, too. Our blue crabs, whose meat is increasingly becoming available throughout the rest of the country, are sweeter and more delicate, and less stringy, than the crabs found most other places. Gulf oysters are another delicacy, and nowhere so good as along the Louisiana coast—large but not too large, the muscle fat and firm enough that you can cut it without the oyster losing its substance, the flavor strong enough in character to stand up to the roux-based sauces of Oysters Edele, but not overpowering. Our beautiful big white Gulf shrimp are responsible for making Louisiana No. 1 in tonnage in United States seafood production. They're available to us locally with the heads still on, and if you can get them that way, too, by all means buy them—the flavor of the shrimp will be incomparable, and the heads will give extra richness to your stock. And redfish, of course, has become synonymous with Louisiana cooking in recent years.

Of course, fresh fish is nothing new in Louisiana. Our great old restaurants have been serving pompano, speckled trout, and red snapper for decades. But changes in the local economy in recent years have created an interesting new development. As people in other parts of the country started eating more fish, Louisiana fishermen found that they had to ship off more of their catch of well-known fish to meet the demand; consequently, they had less for themselves, and they began to discover the special tastes and textures of the great variety of lesser-known fish for which there was as yet no commercial demand. At the same time, harder times in the general economy meant that household budgets were becoming tighter, and people also began to turn to no-name fish (black drum, amberjack, lemon or cobria fish, mullet from Florida) because they were cheaper. What these people were discovering is really very simple: The name of a fish is not nearly so important as its freshness. Nearly every fish has its particular virtues, and there's a technique in Cajun cooking to make the most of each of them.

So repeat after me: Every chef or home cook is only as good as the quality of his ingredients. Limiting yourself at the outset with poor products is like trying to cook with one hand tied behind your back. And again, don't let yourself be discouraged by the bounty Louisiana enjoys—think of our cooking as an encyclopedia of what can be done when nearly everything is available and then look at what you have and see how you can make the most of it. Also keep in mind that even if you live in Iowa, these days you can probably find fish in your local supermarket that very recently was swimming hundreds of miles away—very likely in Louisiana waters. If it's not there, ask if you can special order it, or consult the list of Sources at the back of the book for businesses that will ship fresh seafood—including crawfish—to you directly. It's a pleasure that no one, no matter how landlocked, should forgo entirely.

❦ BOILED CRAWFISH ❧

This is a big, festive party dish. Good Friday is an important holiday for us, and we always plan this for supper that night, which makes it a lot easier to keep the fast. It's a delicacy made for sharing—in fact, in Cajun country, boiling crawfish for only two people counts as a venial sin.

For the boil:

40 pounds live crawfish
1 cup salt
½ cup ground white pepper
½ cup ground black pepper

½ cup ground red pepper
5 pounds small white onions
12 ears of corn, shucked
5 pounds small new potatoes

Wash the crawfish well and pick out any fish bones or other debris. Fill a great big (40-quart) stockpot a quarter full of water. Add the salt and peppers and bring to a boil. Add the whole onions, the corn, and the new potatoes (it will be easy to remove them later if you put them in a cloth sack). Return to a boil, cover, lower heat to medium, and let cook 8 minutes. Add the crawfish, cover again, and raise heat to high. After steam begins to escape from under the lid, cook 7 minutes more. Remove from the heat and let sit 4 minutes. Do not remove the lid until this point!

Remove the onions, corn, and potatoes to a bowl and drain the crawfish. Place the crawfish in a large insulated container (an ice chest works well, as do the thick waterproof boxes chickens are shipped in, which your butcher may give you for free). Have ready a mixture of:

½ cup ground white pepper
½ cup ground black pepper

½ cup ground red pepper
2 cups salt

Sprinkle over the crawfish and mix them well to coat. Cover and let sit for 7 minutes.

Serve immediately with the onions, corn, new potatoes, and lots of French bread on a large table covered with plenty of paper. When everyone has eaten his fill, everyone "peels for the house." The peeled tails can then be used in a cold crawfish cocktail or salad or for Fried Crawfish the next day.

Serves 8–10.

Note: Most of the salt is not added until after the cooking process because too much salt added during cooking makes the flesh of the crawfish adhere to the shell.

❧ CRAWFISH ÉTOUFFÉE ❧

In Cajun country, crawfish was for a long time considered a poor man's food. The little critters were known as an agricultural pest, and hardly anyone would admit to fixing them at home, let along be brave enough to put them on a restaurant menu. They finally went public in 1935 when a glorious crawfish étouffée was the first dish served at a levee bar around Henderson called Bernard's. Now crawfish are treated with the respect they deserve—in fact, every other year the little Cajun community of Breaux Bridge swells to over 300,000 people when it holds its International Crawfish Festival the first weekend in May.

2 cups (1 pound) butter
3 large onions, chopped fine
2 bell peppers, chopped fine
2 teaspoons salt
3/4 teaspoon ground red pepper
1/2 teaspoon ground black pepper
1/2 teaspoon ground white pepper

2 ounces crawfish fat—or as much as you can get your hands on—fresh or frozen (see Sources)
1 cup water
2 pounds fresh crawfish tails (see Sources)
1 cup finely chopped green onions
1/2 cup finely chopped parsley

Melt the butter in a Dutch oven or other large heavy pot, add the onions and bell peppers, and sauté over medium-high heat. Brown well, being sure to scrape the bottom of the pot frequently to loosen any stuck particles. (You want to caramelize the onions to bring out their sweetness.) This process will take about 45 minutes.

Reduce the heat to medium-low and add the salt, peppers, crawfish fat, and water. Stir well and let simmer 30 minutes more. (You can prepare the dish in advance to this point; about 30 minutes before serving, reheat the mixture over medium-high heat.)

Raise the heat to medium, stir in the crawfish, and cook for 10 minutes. Then add the green onions and parsley and let cook for another 5 minutes. Place generous servings of hot cooked rice in the middle of large flat plates and spoon the crawfish all around.

Serves 6.

❧ SHRIMP AND CRAB ÉTOUFFÉE ❧

Don't think of this as a second-best substitute for Crawfish Étouffée. The flavors of the shrimp and the crab combine magically to make this a first-class dish in its own right. We guarantee you'll think about making it at least once a week.

4–6 large live crabs (we use blue crabs)
½ cup (¼ pound) unsalted butter
2 large yellow onions, chopped fine
2 large bell peppers, chopped fine
3 celery ribs, chopped fine
2–3 pounds medium fresh shrimp, heads on (or 1 pound, heads off)

6 cups water
½ cup peanut-butter-colored roux (see Basics)
2 teaspoons salt
1 teaspoon ground red pepper
1 teaspoon ground black pepper
¾ teaspoon ground white pepper
4–5 shots Tabasco sauce
1 cup chopped green onions
1 cup chopped parsley

Place the crabs in the refrigerator to dull them. In a large Dutch oven or other large heavy pot, melt the butter over medium-high heat. Add the onions, bell peppers, and celery and sauté, stirring often, until the vegetables are very soft, about 45 minutes

While the vegetables are cooking, prepare the crabs, which will still be alive but slowed down from the cold of the refrigerator. Working with one crab at a time (leave the rest in the refrigerator), remove the claws and "fingers" and set them aside. Remove the flap at the base of the back shell, insert a small knife, and pry off the back. There will be some crab "fat" along the sides of the back. Scrape it into a small bowl and discard the back. Remove the gills from the sides of the crab body and discard. Crack the body in half and slice each half in half again horizontally, to expose the meat.

Dehead, peel, and devein the shrimp. Place the shrimp peelings and heads in a 4–6-quart stockpot and add the crab fingers and claws and the water. Bring to a boil over medium-high heat and let boil slowly for 45 minutes. Strain the stock, discarding the shrimp heads and peels and crab claws and fingers.

When the vegetables have finished cooking, add the roux and continue to cook over medium-high heat, stirring constantly until the roux is completely absorbed. Stir in the salt, peppers, Tabasco sauce, and reserved crab fat and let cook 10 minutes longer, stirring often. Stir in 2 cups of the shrimp and crab stock, then add additional stock, a cup at a time, until the mixture reaches the consistency of a heavy bisque. Return to a simmer and let cook over medium-low heat for 30–45 minutes. Add the crab bodies and mix well. Cover, reduce heat to low, and let cook for 30 minutes, stirring often. Add the shrimp, green onions, and parsley and cook uncovered over medium heat until the shrimp turn pink, 5–7 minutes.

Serve over beds of rice, distributing the crab bodies evenly and spooning the étouffée over.

Serves 6–8.

❧ FRIED CRAWFISH ❧

These delectable little creatures can be served as an appetizer or entrée, alongside Crawfish Yvonne (we call that Half-'n'-Half), or any other way your heart desires.

3 eggs
12 ounces beer (not too dark)
2 cups milk
2 cups all-purpose flour
2 tablespoons salt
2 teaspoons ground red pepper

2 teaspoons ground black pepper
2 teaspoons ground white pepper
Oil for deep-frying
2 pounds peeled crawfish tails (see Sources)

In a large bowl, beat together the eggs, beer, and milk. Place the flour in a wide shallow bowl. Mix together the salt and peppers and stir half into each bowl.

Heat at least 3 inches of oil to 375°F in a deep-fryer or large heavy pot. Pour the crawfish into the beer batter and mix well to coat. Remove about a quarter of the crawfish from the batter, using a slotted spoon to allow the excess batter to drain off, and dredge them in the flour mixture. Place them in a frying basket and shake the basket to knock off most, but not all, of the excess flour—a little extra is necessary to help the crawfish "bloom" as they fry. Fry the crawfish in the basket until they are firm and golden brown, 2–3 minutes. Drain on paper toweling. Repeat the dredging and frying process three times for the rest of the crawfish.

Serve with Tartar Sauce (see page 90).

Serves 8–10 as a first course, 4–6 as a main course.

❦ CRAWFISH PIE ❧

Most people outside Cajun country know Crawfish Pie only from Hank Williams's classic, "Down on the Bayou." Try this recipe and you'll understand why he wanted to sing about it.

2 cups (1 pound) butter
2 large onions, chopped fine
1 medium bell pepper, chopped
  fine
8 ounces crawfish fat, or as much
  as you can get your hands on,
  fresh or frozen (see Sources)
2 teaspoons salt
1/2 teaspoon ground red pepper

1/2 teaspoon ground black pepper
1/2 teaspoon ground white pepper
1 cup water
1 tablespoon peanut-butter-colored
  roux (see Basics)
2 pounds fresh crawfish (see
  Sources)
1 cup finely chopped green onions
1/2 cup finely chopped parsley

In a Dutch oven or other large heavy pot, melt the butter over high heat and add the onions and bell pepper. Sauté for 20 minutes, stirring often. Reduce heat to low and let cook, uncovered, until the vegetables are very soft, about 30 minutes. Stir in the crawfish fat, salt, peppers, water, and roux and let cook over medium-low heat for another 30 minutes. Add the crawfish, stir, and let cook for another 10 minutes. Stir in the green onions and parsley and remove from heat. Let cool completely, then refrigerate for at least 4 hours, preferably overnight.

Pastry

3 cups flour
2 teaspoons salt
1 1/2 teaspoons sugar

About 9 tablespoons solid
  vegetable shortening
1 cup ice water

Stir together the flour, salt, and sugar. Cut in 3 tablespoons of the shortening. Add the water slowly, mixing well with a fork or your fingers, to make a firm dough. Refrigerate for 30 minutes.

Turn the dough out onto a lightly floured surface and roll into a large rectangle about ¼ inch thick. Spread about 2 tablespoons of the shortening over the surface, then fold each side in toward the center like a napkin, to make three layers. Return dough to the refrigerator for another 30 minutes. Repeat this process twice more, rolling the dough out, spreading it with shortening, folding in thirds, and letting rest in the refrigerator for 30 minutes.

Preheat the oven to 350°F. Roll out two thirds of the pastry about ¼ inch thick on a lightly floured surface and line a 9-inch pie pan with it. (Or you can make individual shells.) Fill the shell three-quarters full with the cold crawfish mixture. Roll out the remaining dough and cut into ½-inch strips. Lay the strips in a lattice pattern on top of the filling, pinching around the edges of the pie to keep them in place. Bake the pie for 45 minutes, or until the pastry is golden brown. Serve hot.

Serves 8–10 as a first course, 4–6 as a main course.

❦ CRAWFISH YVONNE ❧

Yvonne—my grandmother, the matriarch of the Patout family—gave this dish its name. It's a cross between an étouffée and a crawfish stew, and the New Orleans *Times-Picayune* called it "one of the best crawfish dishes in Louisiana."

1¹/₂ cup peanut-butter-colored roux (see Basics)
2 cups (1 pound) butter
4 medium onions, chopped fine
3 medium bell peppers, chopped fine
3 celery ribs, chopped fine
3 pounds peeled crawfish tails (see Sources)
Crawfish fat—as much as possible, but at least 3 ounces (see Sources)

5 cups water
1 tablespoon salt
2 teaspoons ground red pepper
1 teaspoon ground white pepper
1 teaspoon ground black pepper
5–6 drops Tabasco sauce
1 cup chopped green onions
1 cup chopped parsley

(If you are making the roux from scratch, use ¹/₂ cup margarine instead of the oil, and ²/₃ cup flour.)

In a heavy 6–8-quart pot, melt the butter over high heat. Add the onions, bell peppers, and celery and cook, stirring often, until the vegetables are very soft, 30–45 minutes.

While the vegetables are cooking, place the crawfish tails in a large bowl and add the water. Agitate thoroughly with your hands to rinse the crawfish and to separate any remaining fat from them. Pick out any veins or other debris. Drain the crawfish, reserving the liquid, and place the tails in a separate bowls.

Lower the heat under the vegetable mixture and add the roux, salt, peppers, and Tabasco sauce. Cook over medium heat, stirring constantly, until the roux is completely blended in, 3–4 minutes. Stir in the crawfish fat and let the mixture simmer 4–5 minutes more, stirring frequently. If the oil begins to separate out, just stir it back in until the mixture is smooth.

Pour in the crawfish liquid and bring to a heavy simmer. Cook for 10 minutes, stirring often to keep the oil from separating. (You can prepare ahead to this point; return the mixture to a simmer when you are ready to proceed.)

Add the crawfish tails and simmer for 5 minutes. Stir in the green onions and parsley and simmer for 1 minute more. Serve in bowls over rice.

Serves 10.

❧ CRAWFISH BISQUE ☙

For this dish, the saying goes, you need either three days or two families—large Cajun families. One good time to make it is after you've had a big crawfish boil and have all those nice peeled tails ready to go. You may have leftover bisque too, but it will be delicious, and you'll have discovered the ecstasy of a week-long crawfish binge.

1 sack (40 pounds) live crawfish
  (see Sources)
3 large onions, chopped fine
2 medium bell peppers,
  chopped fine
2 celery ribs, chopped fine
2¹/₂–3 cups peanut-butter-colored
  roux (see Basics)

1 tablespoon salt
2 teaspoons ground white
  pepper
1 teaspoon ground red pepper
1 teaspoon ground black
  pepper
1 cup chopped green onions
¹/₂ cup chopped parsley

Fill a large (8-gallon) stockpot one-third full with water. Bring to a heavy boil over high heat and pour in the crawfish. Cover. As soon as steam begins to escape from under the lid, turn the heat off and remove the crawfish. (This will be easier if you place the crawfish in a wire basket to cook them.) Spread them on a large surface covered with paper and let cool.

When the crawfish are cool enough to handle, separate the heads and the claws from the tails. Using a small spoon or your finger, remove the "fat" from the heads and reserve it in a bowl. Reach inside the heads to remove the mud pockets from between the eyes and discard. Place the claws and three quarters of the heads in a 6–8-quart stockpot and add water to cover. Bring to a boil and let boil over medium heat for about 1 hour. Strain the stock; let it cool; discard the claws and heads.

While the stock is boiling, peel the crawfish tails. Discard the peels and reserve the tails.

Prepare the Stuffed Heads (see following recipe).

Return the crawfish stock to a boil over medium-high heat and add the onions, bell peppers, and celery. Reduce heat and let simmer 15–20 minutes. Stir in just enough roux to make a mixture thicker than a soup but thinner than a typical gumbo (don't think of "bisque" in the usual sense). Stir in three quarters of the reserved crawfish fat and the salt and peppers and let simmer for 45 minutes to 1 hour. The bisque can be prepared in advance to this point and stored in the refrigerator, where it will keep well for 2–3 days.

About 20 minutes before serving, return the bisque to a simmer, add the remaining crawfish tails (those not used in the Stuffed Heads) and let simmer for 5 minutes. Add the Stuffed Heads, return to a boil, and let simmer for 15 minutes. Stir in the green onions and parsley, remove from the heat, and serve immediately, distributing the heads and tails evenly among the bowls.

Serves 8–10.

❧ STUFFED HEADS ❧

*Half the cooked, peeled crawfish
  tails from Crawfish Bisque*
2 cups (1 pound) butter
5 large onions, chopped fine
*4 large bell peppers,
  chopped fine*
3 celery ribs, chopped fine
1 tablespoon salt
2 teaspoons ground red pepper
1 teaspoon ground black pepper
1 teaspoon ground white pepper

*Remaining quarter of the crawfish
  fat from Crawfish Bisque*
2 cups bread crumbs
¹/₂ cup chopped green onions
¹/₂ cup chopped parsley
Tabasco sauce to taste
*One-quarter of the cooked, cooled
  crawfish heads from Crawfish
  Bisque*
*Flour for dredging (about 2
  cups)*

Chop the crawfish tails medium fine and reserve. Melt the butter in a Dutch oven or other large heavy pot over medium-high heat and add the onions, bell peppers, and celery. Sauté, stirring often, until very soft, 30–40 minutes. Add the salt and peppers and cook 5–7 minutes more. Stir in a quarter of the crawfish fat and cook for another 10 minutes. Add the chopped crawfish tails, reduce heat to medium, and cook 10–15 minutes more. Remove from heat and stir in the bread crumbs to make a very stiff dressing. Stir in the green onions, parsley, and Tabasco sauce, transfer to a separate container, and let cool. The dressing can be prepared 2–3 days in advance and stored in the refrigerator. If you want to stuff the heads immediately, you can accelerate the cooling process by placing the hot dressing directly in the refrigerator and stirring it every 30 minutes until completely cooled.

To stuff the heads: Hold a crawfish head in one hand. With the other hand, using a spoon or your fingers, stuff the cavity, packing the dressing so that it does not protrude beyond the shell. Place the flour in a flat pan and roll the heads in it lengthwise, so that both the exposed ends are coated, but not all of the shell is. (Too much flour on the heads will make the bisque too thick.) Place the stuffed heads on cookie sheets, dressing side up, as you finish them.

(This whole process goes a lot faster with a three- or four-person assembly line.)

Preheat the oven to 375°F. Bake the heads for 20 minutes, then place them under the broiler for 3–4 minutes to brown the tops. Transfer the heads to a separate container and let them cool. (The heads can also be prepared 2–3 days in advance).

❧ CRAWFISH STUFFED BELL PEPPERS ❧

The dressing we use for the Stuffed Heads in our Crawfish Bisque is so terrific that you'll want to find other uses for it, especially when you don't have time to make the bisque. Here it's used to stuff bell peppers that work wonderfully as an appetizer or main course.

Crawfish dressing from Crawfish   *4–5 bell peppers*
   Bisque (page 65)   *Grated Parmesan cheese*

If you are making the crawfish dressing from scratch, use 2 pounds crawfish tails. Let the dressing cool completely.

Preheat the oven to 325°F. Cut off the stems of the peppers at the base and halve and seed them. Bring a large pot of water to a heavy boil, drop in the pepper halves, and parboil them for 3–4 minutes. Drain and let cool. Stuff the pepper halves generously with the crawfish dressing, mounding it nicely. Place the peppers in an ovenproof dish or pan large enough to hold them comfortably in a single layer. Bake for 25 minutes, or until the peppers are tender and the tops are lightly browned. Sprinkle with Parmesan cheese and place under the broiler briefly to glaze. Serve immediately.

Serves 8–10 as an appetizer, 4–5 as a main course.

❧ BOILED CRABS ❧

When we talk about boiled crabs in my family, two people come to mind—Mo Mo (my father's mother, Yvonne) and my sister Gigi. They could eat boiled crabs seven days a week, twenty-four hours a day, and not get tired of them. When you try this recipe, you'll see why.

2 lemons, quartered or sliced
8 new red potatoes
4 small ears fresh corn
4 small yellow onions
1 cup salt

1/2 cup ground red pepper
1/2 cup ground white pepper
1/2 cup ground black pepper
1 dozen live blue (or other small to medium) crabs

Fill a large (10-quart) stockpot one-third full with water. Add the lemons, potatoes, corn, onions, salt, and peppers. Cover and bring to a boil over high heat. Let boil for 10 minutes. Add the crabs, cover, and return to a boil. Once steam starts to escape from under the cover, let cook for 15 minutes. Turn off the heat and let sit, covered, for 10 minutes more.

We like to lay out the crabs and vegetables on a large table covered with lots of paper and have a feast.

Serves 2 Cajuns, 4 elsewhere.

CRAB EUGENE

This crab dressing is one of the foundations of Cajun cooking. In fact, it is named after our founder, Papa Eugene. Once you master it, you'll be able to use it in all kinds of dishes—stuffed peppers, mushrooms, crabs, fish, and so on. The recipe does not work as well in less than the amount given, so if you need less than a full batch, freeze the extra.

Crab Dressing

1 cup (¹/₂ pound) butter
3 large onions, chopped coarse
2 bell peppers, chopped coarse
2 celery ribs, chopped coarse
1–2 cups crab fat (optional; see Sources)
Juice of 3 fresh lemons or ¹/₄ cup lemon juice
¹/₄ cup Worcestershire sauce
1 tablespoon salt
2 teaspoons ground red pepper

1 teaspoon ground white pepper
2 teaspoons ground black pepper
2 pounds crab meat (white or claw)
¹/₂ loaf French bread (day-old is fine)
2 cups water or seafood stock
1 cup chopped green onions
1 cup chopped parsley

Melt the butter over medium-high heat, add the onions, bell peppers, celery, crab fat, lemon juice, Worcestershire, and seasonings. Cook, stirring occasionally, until the vegetables are very soft (45 minutes or more). Add the crab meat and cook 5 minutes longer.

While the vegetables are cooking, slice the bread thin and place it on a cookie sheet in a low oven (200°F) to dry out—this will take up to 30 minutes (don't let it brown). Place the dry bread in a bowl and work in enough stock or water to make a very thick mash.

Reduce the heat under the vegetable-crab mixture to low, mix in the bread mash, and continue to cook, stirring constantly, until the mixture is completely homogenized. Remove from the heat, stir in the green onions and parsley, and let cool. Refrigerate for at least 2 hours.(If you live in a warm climate, it's a good idea to speed up the cooling process by transferring the hot dressing to a shallow pan and placing it directly in the refrigerator.) You can prepare the dressing up to 4 days in advance. It also freezes well.

Assembly

Butter   *Bread crumbs*
Lemon juice

Butter 6 individual 8-ounce ramekins, soufflé dishes, or custard cups (crab or scallop shells make a very nice presentation if you can get them—you will probably need twice as many, since they hold less). Divide the dressing evenly among them, drizzle about a teaspoonful of lemon juice over each, and sprinkle generously with bread crumbs. Place on a cookie sheet and bake at 375°F for 15–20 minutes. You can glaze them under the broiler for a couple of minutes if you like. Serve immediately.

Serves 6.

❧ STUFFED BELL PEPPERS ❧

6 large bell peppers   *Lemon juice*
1 recipe Crab Dressing (see page   *Bread crumbs*
  70)

Halve the peppers lengthwise but do not stem them. Remove the seeds. Bring a large kettle of water to a boil, drop in the peppers, return to a boil, and cook for 2–3 minutes. Drain.

Lay the pepper halves, cavities up, in a baking pan just large enough to hold them in a single layer. Divide the dressing equally among them. Drizzle about a teaspoon of lemon juice over each and sprinkle generously with bread crumbs. Place in a preheated 350°F oven and bake for 15–20 minutes, until the peppers are tender and the dressing is heated through. If you like, you can glaze them under the broiler for a minute or two before serving.

Serves 6.

🦐 STUFFED SHRIMP 🦐

2 pounds large fresh shrimp,
  heads off
$^1/_2$ recipe Crab Dressing (see page
  70)
3 tablespoons salt
3 teaspoons ground red pepper
2 teaspoons ground black pepper

2 teaspoons ground white pepper
2 cups all-purpose flour
2 cups corn flour
3 eggs
2 cups milk
12 ounces beer (not too dark)
Oil for deep-frying

Peel the shrimp but leave the tails on. Butterfly them by slitting them down the back, removing the vein, and cutting almost all the way through down to the base of the tail, so that they lie flat. Place a heaping tablespoon of the dressing in the middle of each shrimp, then press the sides of the shrimp so that they adhere to the dressing.

In a small bowl, mix together the salt and peppers. Place the flour and corn flour separately in two wide shallow bowls. In a mixing bowl, whisk together the eggs, milk, and beer. Divide the salt-pepper mixture evenly among the flour, corn flour, and beer batter and mix well.

Heat at least 3 inches of oil in a fryer or deep kettle to 350°F. Dredge each shrimp in the flour, dip in the beer batter, then dredge in the corn flour, making sure that the dressing is completely covered (pat the corn flour on to be sure it adheres). Fry the shrimp for 3–5 minutes, until they are a nice golden brown. Drain on paper toweling. (It's best to work with no more than half a dozen shrimp at a time, from dredging to frying, to prevent the dressing from soaking through.) Serve with Tartar Sauce (see page 90).

Serves 6.

FRIED SHRIMP

Allow 2–3 pounds medium to large shrimp for 6 people. Peel and devein them but leave the tails on. Dredge and fry as above (you can dredge more lightly since there is no stuffing). These will take a little less time to fry, 4–5 minutes.

❧ CAJUN EGGPLANT DRESSING ❧

This is one of those basic Cajun recipes from which you can create an infinite number of dishes. You can bake it in a casserole or in individual ramekins, or you can shoot the works and use it to stuff pirogues—deep-fried eggplant boats. In its simplest form, it may not be all that pretty, but—*cher*, that flavor.

2 pounds medium fresh shrimp,
 heads off
4 cups water
1 cup (½ pound) margarine
3 large onions, chopped fine
2 medium bell peppers, chopped
 fine
2 celery ribs, chopped fine
4 medium eggplants
1½ teaspoons ground red pepper
1½ teaspoons ground white pepper
1½ teaspoons ground black pepper
1½ tablespoons salt

4–6 dashes Tabasco sauce
1 teaspoon dried thyme, or 1
 tablespoon fresh
1 teaspoon dried basil, or 1
 tablespoon fresh
½ teaspoon dried oregano, or 2
 teaspoons fresh
1 pound cooked crab meat, claw
 or white
1 cup chopped green onions
1 cup chopped parsley
Grated Parmesan cheese
Bread crumbs

Peel and devein the shrimp; set aside. Place the peels in a small saucepan and add the water. Bring to a boil and reduce by half over medium-high heat, 15–20 minutes. Strain and set aside.

Melt the margarine over medium-high heat in a Dutch oven or other large heavy pot and add the onions, peppers, and celery. Cook the vegetables until they are very soft, stirring occasionally, 30–45 minutes.

Meanwhile, peel the eggplants and cut them into 1-inch cubes. Place them in a saucepan and add water to cover. Bring to a boil and boil slowly for a few minutes, just until tender. Drain. Puree until smooth in a blender or food processor, or put through a ricer.

Add the eggplant, shrimp stock, seasonings, and herbs to the vegetable mixture, return to a simmer, and cook over medium heat for 10 minutes, stirring occasionally. Add the shrimp and continue to cook over medium-high heat just until the shrimp turn pink, 5–7 minutes. Add the crab meat and cook just long enough to heat through. Remove from the heat and stir in the green onions and parsley. (This much can be done in advance.)

Spoon the hot dressing into a casserole or individual ramekins. Sprinkle generously with Parmesan cheese and bread crumbs and glaze under the broiler for a couple of minutes. (If you have made the dressing ahead, place the casserole in a preheated 350°F oven for 45 minutes or so to warm through before glazing; ramekins will take only 15–20 minutes.)

Serves 6–8.

❧ STUFFED EGGPLANT ❧

1 recipe Cajun Eggplant Dressing
  (see page 73)
6 medium eggplants
3 eggs
2 cups milk
12 ounces beer (not too dark)
3 cups all-purpose flour

2 teaspoons salt
1 teaspoon ground red pepper
1 teaspoon ground black pepper
1 teaspoon ground white pepper
Oil for deep-frying
Grated Parmesan cheese
Bread crumbs

Make the eggplant dressing as directed, using the flesh from the 6 eggplants, which you obtain as follows:

Peel the whole eggplants and slice off an even third of each, lengthwise. Remove a thin slice from the opposite side as well, to keep them from rolling. Remove as much of the flesh as possible from the inside, leaving a "boat" about ½ inch thick. Place them in a large bowl and immediately cover with water to keep them from browning. (You can refrigerate the shells this way for 2–3 days, along with the dressing, if you want to prepare in advance.) Prepare the eggplant dressing with the scooped-out flesh and the reserved eggplant thirds, but do not put it in casseroles.

Beat the eggs in a bowl with the milk and beer. Place the flour in a wide shallow bowl. Combine the salt and peppers and stir half into each.

Heat at least 5 inches of oil in a deep-fryer or other large heavy pot to 350°F. Drain the eggplants and pat them dry. Dip them first into the beer batter, then into the flour, covering them well inside and out. Shake off the excess flour. Fry the eggplant boats, two at a time, until nicely browned, 6–8 minutes. Drain on paper toweling.

Place the eggplant shells side by side on a cookie sheet or in a shallow baking pan. Be sure the eggplant dressing is good and hot. Divide it equally among the boats and sprinkle generously with Parmesan cheese and bread crumbs. Glaze under the broiler for a minute or two before serving.

Serves 6–8.

❧ FRIED SOFT-SHELL CRABS ❧

One of the sea's real treasures, to my mind, is soft-shell crabs, which are abundant along the Gulf Coast around April and September and at other times of the year in other parts of the country. For a real gourmet treat that plays up the sweetness of the crabs with a creamy lump crab meat sauce, try the Soft-Shell Crabs Elizabeth.

8–10 fresh soft-shell crabs
1 tablespoon salt
2 teaspoons ground black pepper
1½ teaspoons ground red pepper
1 teaspoon ground white pepper
3 eggs

12 ounces beer (not too
dark)
2 cups milk
2 cups all-purpose flour
3 cups corn flour
Vegetable oil for deep-frying

Clean the crabs: Lift the pointed sides and remove the lungs or gills on each side with a small sharp knife, then remove the mud pockets located between the eyes.

In a small bowl, mix together the salt and peppers. In a separate bowl, beat together the eggs, beer, milk, and one third of the salt-pepper mixture. Divide the rest of the salt-pepper mixture equally between the flour and corn flour and place them in separate large flat pans.

Pour oil into a Dutch oven or other large heavy pot to a depth of at least 3 inches. Place over medium-high heat and heat to 350°F. Working with three or four crabs at a time (that's all the pot will be able to handle), dredge them gently in the flour on both sides, then dip in the beer batter, then dredge in the corn flour, lifting the side flaps to coat well. Shake off any excess flour and place immediately in the hot oil. (Don't try to batter the crabs ahead—their high water content will destroy the coating in no time.) Fry the crabs until they are nicely browned, 4–5 minutes, turning once. Drain on paper toweling and serve immediately, plain or with cocktail sauce or Tartar Sauce (see page 90).

Serves 4–5.

❧ SOFT-SHELL CRABS ELIZABETH ☙

1½ cups heavy cream	½ teaspoon ground black pepper
2 teaspoons fresh basil, or	¼ teaspoon ground white pepper
½ teaspoon dried	½ recipe Fried Soft-Shell Crabs
2 teaspoons fresh thyme, or	(see preceding recipe)
½ teaspoon dried	1 pound fresh lump crab meat
1 teaspoon salt	¼ cup chopped green onions
½ teaspoon ground red pepper	¼ cup chopped parsley

Place the cream in a large heavy skillet and bring to a simmer over medium-high heat, stirring often. Stir in the herbs and seasonings and let reduce until you have a nice thick sauce that coats the spoon heavily, 10–15 minutes.

While the cream sauce is reducing, fry the crabs as directed above and drain them on paper toweling.

As soon as the crabs are finished, add the lump crab meat and the green onions and parsley to the cream sauce and let simmer 2–3 minutes more. Stir gently—you don't want to break up the crab meat too much. Place one crab on each plate and spoon the sauce equally over each.

Serves 4–5.

☙ SHRIMP CREOLE ❧

This recipe must have been made in heaven, because its magic comes from two ingredients that just happen to come in season at the same time—shrimp and fresh tomatoes. And the Jambalaya is a Cajun's way of not letting any of nature's nice coincidences go to waste. It uses Shrimp Creole as a base (leftovers work fine), to give you a delicious and entirely different main dish.

3 pounds medium fresh shrimp, heads on (or 2 pounds, heads off)
1 quart water
1/2 cup vegetable oil
3 medium yellow onions, chopped
2 large bell peppers, chopped
5 celery ribs, chopped fine
8–10 large fresh tomatoes, peeled, seeded, and roughly chopped
2 teaspoons salt

1 teaspoon ground red pepper
1/2 teaspoon ground black pepper
1/2 teaspoon ground white pepper
1 tablespoon fresh thyme, or 2 teaspoons dried
1 tablespoon fresh basil, or 2 teaspoons dried
1–1 1/2 teaspoons sugar
4–5 bay leaves
1 cup chopped green onions
1 cup chopped parsley

Dehead, peel, and devein the shrimp. Place the heads and peels in a small saucepan and add the water. Bring to a slow boil over medium-high heat and let boil slowly for 15–20 minutes. Strain and discard the heads and peels.

Place the oil in a Dutch oven or other large, heavy pot and place over medium-high heat. Add the onions, peppers, and celery and sauté, stirring often, until the vegetables are very soft, about 45 minutes. Stir in the tomatoes, salt, peppers, herbs, sugar, and shrimp stock and return to a simmer. Reduce the heat to medium and let simmer for 2 hours, stirring occasionally. This is your Creole sauce; it can be prepared 1 or 2 days in advance and stored in the refrigerator.

When you are ready to serve, return the sauce to a simmer and add the shrimp. Cook until they turn pink, 5–7 minutes. Stir in the green onions and parsley and let cook 1 minute more. Serve on flat plates over beds of rice.

Serves 6–8.

SHRIMP AND HAM OR TASSO JAMBALAYA

Prepare Shrimp Creole as above, but add about a pound of cubed ham and a 4-ounce can of tomato sauce to the finished sauce and simmer 45 minutes more. Meanwhile, boil or steam 2–3 cups raw rice. Finish the sauce (which will be your jambalaya base) by adding the shrimp, green onions, and parsley as above. (If you are using leftover Shrimp Creole, remove the shrimp, then reheat the sauce, add the ham and tomato sauce, and proceed as above. Return the shrimp to the pan at the end of cooking.) Place the hot, cooked rice in a large bowl, pour the jambalaya base over, mix well, and serve.

You can also prepare this with sausage instead of ham.

❧ SHRIMP MS. ANN ❧

This delectable dish is named for my mother, who created it at our "camp" at Cypremort Point. It's very adaptable—you can sauté the shrimp, or broil or bake them.

2 pounds large shrimp, heads off
2 teaspoons salt
1/2 teaspoon ground red pepper
1/4 teaspoon ground black pepper
1/4 teaspoon ground white pepper
1 cup (1/2 pound) butter

1/4 cup dry vermouth
1/2 cup lemon juice or 2 fresh
  lemons
1/4 cup Worcestershire sauce
1/2 cup chopped green onions
1/2 cup chopped parsley

Peel the shrimp and devein them, but leave the tails on. Sprinkle generously with the salt and peppers, mixing well, and arrange in a single layer in a baking pan.

Melt the butter over medium heat and add the vermouth, lemon juice, Worcestershire, green onions, and parsley. Simmer for 3 minutes, then pour over the shrimp.

Bake the shrimp in a preheated 375°F oven just until they turn pink, 10–15 minutes. (You can also broil them, which will take less time.)

Serves 6–8 as a first course, 4 as a main dish.

❧ OYSTERS GIGI ❧

This dish, named for the elder of my two sisters, Eugenie (known as Gigi), is as easy as it is wonderful. It works especially well as an appetizer.

12 strips of bacon	*3 eggs*
2 dozen fresh shucked oysters, drained	*12 ounces beer (not too dark)*
2 teaspoons salt	*2 cups flour*
1 teaspoon ground red pepper	*2 cups seasoned Italian bread crumbs*
1 teaspoon ground black pepper	*Vegetable oil for deep-frying*
1/2 teaspoon ground white pepper	

Halve the bacon slices and fry them until until they become transparent and begin to render their fat, about 2 minutes. Wrap a half strip of bacon around each oyster and secure with a toothpick. In a small bowl, mix together the salt and peppers; set aside. In a separate bowl, beat together the eggs and beer and half of the salt-pepper mixture. Mix together the flour and the remaining salt-pepper mixture and place in a large flat pan. Place the bread crumbs in another large flat pan.

Pour oil into a Dutch oven or other large heavy pot and heat to 375°F. Roll the bacon-wrapped oysters in the seasoned flour to coat them well, then dip them in the beer batter, stirring to coat, then roll them in the bread crumbs. (Do all the oysters at once.) Deep-fry the oysters in the hot oil until they are well browned, 2–3 minutes. Don't crowd the pot—fry in batches if you need to. Drain on paper toweling and serve plain or with Tartar Sauce (see page 90) or cocktail sauce.

Serves 6 as a first course, 4 as a main course.

❧ OYSTERS ALEXANDER ❧

Oysters Alexander are guaranteed to make Oysters Bienville and Rockefeller obsolete. This recipe really requires the full amount of oyster liquor. It is worth shucking the oysters yourself to get it if you can't buy it. If you end up with more than you need, I'll explain how to work the extra in to give the dish an even stronger oyster flavor.

1 cup (½ pound) margarine
3 medium onions, chopped fine
1 medium bell pepper, chopped fine
1 celery rib, chopped fine
2 garlic cloves, minced
½ loaf French bread (day-old is fine)
3 cups oyster liquor
1 pound medium fresh shrimp, heads off
3 pints unwashed shucked oysters

2 teaspoons dried thyme, or 1 tablespoon fresh
2 teaspoons dried basil, or 1 tablespoon fresh
6 drops Tabasco sauce
1 tablespoon salt
2 teaspoons ground red pepper
1 teaspoon ground white pepper
1 teaspoon ground black pepper
1 cup sliced green onions
1 cup chopped parsley
24 cleaned oyster shells or small (4-ounce) ramekins
Grated Parmesan cheese

Melt the margarine in a heavy 4–6-quart pot over medium-high heat. Add the onions, bell pepper, celery, and garlic and cook until the vegetables are very soft, 45 minutes to 1 hour, stirring occasionally. (If you have extra oyster liquor, add it at the end of this time and continue cooking for a few minutes to evaporate the extra liquid.)

Slice the bread thin. Place the slices on a cookie sheet and put them in a preheated 200°F oven to dry out thoroughly, which will take up to 30 minutes (don't let them brown). Place the bread in a bowl, pour the oysters liquor over, and set aside to soak.

Peel and devein the shrimp and cut them in thirds. Cut all the oysters in half through the muscle, except 2 dozen for the stuffing.

Add the shrimp and herbs to the vegetable mixture. Mix together the salt and peppers and add all but a teaspoon; continue to cook over medium-high heat just until the shrimp turn pink, 4–5 minutes. Then add the oysters and cook just until they curl around the edges. Thoroughly mash together the reserved bread and oyster liquor and add in. Reduce the heat to low and cook, stirring constantly, until a smooth consistency is reached. Remove from the heat and stir in the green onions and the parsley. Let cool and refrigerate for at least 2 hours. (If you live in a warm climate, it's a good idea to speed up the cooling process by transferring the hot dressing to a shallow pan and placing it directly in the refrigerator.)

Lay out the oyster shells or ramekins on a cookie sheet. Place an oyster in each and sprinkle with the reserved salt and peppers. Divide the oyster dressing evenly among the shells or ramekins, mounding slightly. Bake in a preheated 375°F oven for 25–30 minutes. Sprinkle generously with Parmesan cheese and place under the broiler to glaze for a minute or two before serving.

Serves 10–12 as a first course, or 6 as a main course.

❧ FRIED OYSTERS ☙

There's no one right way to fry oysters, but there are a few secrets that will help you make them perfectly. Don't batter them up ahead of time, and be sure the oil is good and hot before you fry them. You'll be surprised at the difference it makes.

1 tablespoon salt	*3 eggs*
2 teaspoons ground red pepper	*2 cups cornmeal*
2 teaspoons ground black pepper	*2 cups corn flour*
1 teaspoon ground white pepper	*Oil for deep-frying*
2 cups milk	*4 dozen fresh shucked oysters*

In a small bowl, mix together the salt and peppers; set aside. In a separate bowl, beat together the milk, eggs, and half the salt-pepper mixture. Mix together the cornmeal, corn flour, and the remaining salt-pepper mixture and place in a large flat pan.

Pour at least 3 inches of oil into a Dutch oven or other large heavy pot and heat to 375°F. Place the oysters in the milk batter, stirring to coat well, then roll them in the cornmeal mixture. Place them in a frying basket and shake gently to get rid of any excess coating. Place the basket in the hot oil and fry the oysters until well browned, 3–4 minutes. Unless your pot is very large, you will probably need to fry this quantity of oysters in two or three batches so as not to crowd them. Drain the oysters on paper toweling and serve immediately, plain or with Tartar Sauce (see page 90) or cocktail sauce.

Serves 6–8.

❦ PASTA WITH OYSTERS AND TASSO ❧

If you're fond of smoked oysters, you'll love this recipe. The fresh oysters stay nice and plump, and the dish gets its smoky flavor from the tasso or other smoked ham. With pasta a perennial favorite in American households these days, you'll want to try this recipe with shrimp, scallops, or crawfish instead of the oysters and enjoy it year-round.

1 pint heavy cream
1/2 pound tasso or other smoked cured ham, such as Smithfield, diced
3/4 teaspoon salt
1/4 teaspoon ground black pepper
1/4 teaspoon ground red pepper
1/4 teaspoon ground white pepper

2 teaspoons fresh basil, or 1/2 teaspoon dried
2 teaspoons fresh thyme, or 1/2 teaspoon dried
1 pound spaghetti, fresh if possible
2 dozen fresh shucked oysters
1/2 cup chopped green onions
1/2 cup chopped parsley

Pour the cream into a large heavy skillet and place over medium heat. Stir the cream when it begins to rise to keep it from overflowing; when it comes to a boil, add the tasso, salt, peppers, and herbs and let simmer for 8–10 minutes. The cream sauce should be quite thick because the liquid from the oysters will thin it out. You can prepare the sauce ahead to this point.

Bring a large pot of salted water to a rolling boil and drop in the pasta. Cook just until al dente. Meanwhile, return the sauce to a simmer, stir in the oysters, green onions, and parsley and cook just until the oysters curl around the edges, 3–4 minutes. Drain the pasta and divide among bowls. Spoon the sauce over and serve with Parmesan cheese.

Serves 4–6.

❧ STUFFED FISH ❧

Almost any very fresh fish—saltwater or freshwater—will work for this recipe: speckled trout, redfish, red snapper, pompano, lemonfish, bass, striped bass, and so on. You can use a big beautiful red snapper with the spine and outer fins removed and the head and tail left on, stuffing the dressing between the two big fillets. Or you can stuff individual fillets. Your imagination's your limit.

3 pounds fresh fish fillets, or one 10–15-pound whole fish
Salt
Ground red pepper
Ground white pepper
Ground black pepper
1 recipe Crab Dressing (see page 70)
1 cup (½ pound) butter

½ cup lemon juice or 1 fresh lemon
¼ cup Worcestershire sauce
⅛ cup dry vermouth
½ chopped green onions
½ cup chopped parsley
Paprika (for individual fillets only)

If you are using a whole fish, remove the dorsal fin and the spine from the base of the head to the tail (on most fish you can do this by cutting through the spine at the head and tail and sliding a knife through the back and down along each side of the spine). Sprinkle inside and out with salt and the peppers. Spoon the crab dressing into the cavity, being sure it is entirely covered by the top fillet. Place the fish in a shallow ovenproof dish large enough to leave ½ to 1 inch space all around.

If you are using individual fillets, slice them into thin 2-ounce fillets (you should have 24 in all). Sprinkle them with salt and the peppers. For each serving, place 2 fillets side by side in a baking dish that will hold 12 servings this size, with ½ to 1 inch space around the edge. Mound the dressing equally over each pair of fillets. Cover each portion with 2 more fillets, making sure the dressing is completely covered.

Melt the butter over medium-high heat, add the lemon juice, Worcestershire, vermouth, green onions, and parsley, and simmer for 3 minutes. Pour evenly over the fish. If you are using fillets, sprinkle them with paprika. Bake in a preheated over (350°F for a whole fish, 375°F for fillets) and bake until the fish flakes. (A whole fish will take about 1½ hours, fillets about 45 minutes. Don't be afraid to lift up the fish to check.)

It's a nice touch to glaze the fish under the broiler for a couple of minutes at the end.

Serves 12.

❧ BAKED FISH WITH CREOLE SAUCE ❧

In Louisiana, we like to mix and match the elements of different recipes to get the best of all possible worlds. Here, moist, delicious baked fish meets the spiciness of the Creole sauce we traditionally use with shrimp. Stuffed fish, by the way, is also excellent prepared with a Creole sauce.

1 recipe Creole sauce (see Shrimp Creole, page 78)
1 large (8-pound) saltwater fish (we use redfish, snapper, grouper, and lemonfish, among others)

2 teaspoons salt
1 teaspoon ground red pepper
½ teaspoon ground black pepper
½ teaspoon ground white pepper
1 lemon, sliced

Prepare the Creole sauce as for Shrimp Creole, using 2 cups shrimp or fish stock. Let cool.

Preheat the oven to 350°F. Clean the fish, but leave it whole. I like to leave the head on, too—it helps seal in the juices. Mix together the salt and peppers in a small bowl and rub on all sides of the fish and in the belly. Place the fish in an ovenproof dish large enough to hold it with about ½ inch of space all around. Pour the Creole sauce over and place the lemon slices in a line down the fish from head to tail. Cover well with a lid or foil. Place the fish in the oven and bake for 2½ hours without uncovering. (For a larger fish you'll need to increase the cooking time.)

If you wish, you can transfer the fish to a serving platter, but be very careful—it may take two people. Garnish with lemon and parsley. Or you can serve directly from the pan on individual plates. Serve the flesh above the spine first, then remove the spine and serve the rest, so that your guests won't have to fight bones. Spoon the sauce over and accompany with rice.

Serves 6–8.

☙ FRIED FISH ❧

Fried fish is a Southern—not just a Cajun—specialty, and you can use this method across the Mason-Dixon line as well. Any firm, white-fleshed fish, saltwater or fresh, will do you proud prepared this way.

2 pounds firm, white-fleshed fish
fillets
1 tablespoon salt
2 teaspoons ground red pepper
2 teaspoons ground white pepper
2 teaspoons ground black pepper

3 eggs
2 cups milk
12 ounces beer (not too
dark)
4 cups corn flour
Vegetable oil for deep-frying

If you are using catfish, try to get whole fillets of 2–3 ounces each, so that you don't have to cut them—they're delicate. If you are using larger fillets, cut them into 1- to 2-ounce pieces. Mix the salt and peppers together in a small bowl and set aside. In a medium mixing bowl, beat together the eggs, milk, beer, and half the salt-pepper mixture. Mix the other half of the salt-pepper mixture with the corn flour and place it in a large flat pan. Place the fish chunks in the beer batter and let them soak for at least 15 minutes.

Pour the oil into a Dutch oven or other large heavy pot to a depth of at least 3 inches and heat to 350°F. (If you are frying a lot of fish, add 5 whole garlic cloves to the oil; it will help keep the oil and the fish from picking up a burnt taste.) Transfer the fish to the corn flour mixture and dredge well, patting gently to shake off any excess. Add the fish slowly to the oil, to keep the temperature of the oil from dropping and to avoid splattering. Don't crowd the pot—fry in batches if you have more fish than your pot can handle. Fry the fillets until they are golden brown, 4–5 minutes. (Larger pieces of fish, especially saltwater, will take up to 3 or 4 minutes longer.) Pull out a fillet and break it in two to check whether the fish is cooked. Drain the fish on paper toweling and serve immediately. I like to accompany fried fish with Tartar Sauce and Hush Puppies.

Serves 6–8.

❧ TARTAR SAUCE ❧

*2 cups homemade mayonnaise
  (see page 156)
Juice of 3 lemons*

*2 tablespoons sweet pickle relish
4–5 shots Tabasco sauce
Vinegar (optional)*

In a small mixing bowl, blend together all the ingredients except the vinegar. Taste. If you like your tartar sauce tarter, add more lemon juice and a little vinegar; if you like it sweeter, add more relish; and if you like it hotter, add more Tabasco. But however you like it, please use homemade mayonnaise—it makes all the difference.

Makes 2 cups.

❧ HUSH PUPPIES ❧

*1¹/₂ cups yellow cornmeal
¹/₂ cup all-purpose flour
1 green onion, chopped fine
2 teaspoons double-acting baking
  powder*

*1 teaspoon salt
³/₄ cup milk
1 egg
Vegetable oil for deep-frying*

In a medium mixing bowl, combine the cornmeal, flour, green onion, baking powder, and salt. Beat together the milk and egg in a cup and stir into the dry ingredients, just enough to moisten the dry ingredients thoroughly.

Pour the oil into a heavy skillet or wide pot to a depth of 2–3 inches. Heat to 350°F. Drop the batter by tablespoonfuls into the oil, being careful not to crowd the pot (fry in batches, if necessary).

Fry the hush puppies until crisp and golden, about 2 minutes. Remove with a slotted spoon and drain on paper toweling. Serve hot.

Serves 6–8.

❧ LADY FISH ❧

This is one of the most popular dishes on our menu. It's named for an old friend of the family, Miss Edna Lee Landry, who supplies us with a lot of the fish she catches by herself on her boat out in Vermilion Bay. She didn't want the dish called Redfish Edna Lee, lest people think it was named for her husband's boat, the *Edna Lee*—and that maybe *he* was catching all those fish—so we named it for her boat—the *Lady Fish*.

1 pound medium fresh shrimp, heads off
¹/₂ teaspoon salt
¹/₄ teaspoon ground red pepper
¹/₄ teaspoon ground black pepper
¹/₄ teaspoon ground white pepper
¹/₄ teaspoon dried basil
¹/₄ teaspoon dried thyme
¹/₄ teaspoon paprika
¹/₄ teaspoon granulated garlic

¹/₄ teaspoon oregano
1 cup (¹/₂ pound) butter
Juice of 3 lemons
2 tablespoons Worcestershire sauce
1 tablespoon vermouth
4 redfish fillets, 8 ounces each
1 pound lump crab meat
¹/₂ cup chopped green onions
¹/₂ cup chopped parsley

Preheat a charcoal grill; let it get very hot.

Remove the heads from the shrimp and peel and devein them; reserve. In a small bowl, mix together the salt, peppers, basil, thyme, paprika, garlic, and oregano; set aside. Melt the butter in a medium saucepan over medium heat and add the lemon juice,

Worcestershire, and vermouth; cook 2–3 minutes. Dip the fish in the butter sauce and sprinkle heavily on both sides with the herb and seasoning mixture. Grill for 2–3 minutes on each side, as you would a steak (the grill should be as hot as you can get it). While the fish is cooking, return the butter sauce to a simmer. Add the crab meat, shrimp, green onions, and parsley and cook just until the shrimp turn pink, 2–3 minutes. Place the cooked fish on individual plates and spoon the sauce equally over each serving.

Serves 4.

❧ REDFISH EUGENIE ☙

My sister Gigi—short for Eugenie—took Best of Show at the 1985 Acadiana Culinary Classic with this, an achievement that launched her into national prominence as a chef in her own right. The technique is very simple, and the recipe adapts well to all kinds of firm, white-fleshed fish. If you can't easily get fresh crawfish, try substituting shrimp or make Redfish Elizabeth, using fresh lump crab meat.

2 teaspoons salt
1 teaspoon ground red pepper
1/2 teaspoon ground black pepper
1/2 teaspoon ground white
   pepper
Dash of nutmeg
1 pint heavy cream
1/2 cup chopped green onions
1/2 cup chopped parsley

2 teaspoons dried basil, or 1
   tablespoon fresh
2 teaspoons dried thyme, or 1
   tablespoon fresh
2 pounds peeled crawfish tails
   (see Sources), blanched
6 redfish fillets, 8 ounces each
Flour for dredging
1 (1/2 pound) cup magarine

Mix seasonings in a small bowl. Bring the cream to a boil in a large skillet or saucepan over medium-high heat. Add the green onions, parsley, herbs, and one half of the seasonings and continue cooking down until thick. Test the consistency by dripping from a spoon—the drops should be thick and full, and the last drop should cling to the spoon.

Add the crawfish tails and return to a simmer. The liquid from the crawfish will thin out the sauce, so continue cooking down until the mixture again becomes thick, 5 minutes at most. Keep warm in a bain-marie, if necessary, until the fish is ready.

Pat the fillets dry and sprinkle with the other half of the salt and peppers. Dredge lightly with flour. Heat the margarine in a large skillet over high heat until very hot and pan-fry the fillets until golden brown, turning just once (about 3 minutes on each side).

Place the fillets on individual plates and top with a generous amount of sauce. Be sure you distribute the crawfish evenly!

Serves 6.

REDFISH ELIZABETH

Follow the recipe for Redfish Eugenie, substituting 2 pounds lump crab meat for the crawfish.

☙ TROUT MICHEL ❧

We created this dish when we started getting in a lot of small trout, and named it for my youngest brother, Michel (we call him Mitch), who is in charge of operations at Patout's in New Iberia. The problem was, the trout were so small that they yielded disappointingly small fillets that tended to dry out when they were cooked. So we tried leaving them whole and came up with this super-fast way of cooking them. The bacon keeps the fish from sticking to the skillet or falling apart, and gives a subtle contrast in flavor, and the method gives a perfectly moist result that should work well with other kinds of trout, too. Don't be squeamish about leaving the head on—it really helps seal in the juices.

*4 whole speckled trout, 10–16
    ounces each*
1 tablespoon salt
1 teaspoon ground red pepper
1/2 teaspoon ground black pepper
*1/4 teaspoon ground white
    pepper*
*2 teaspoons fresh basil, or
    1/2 teaspoon dried*

*2 teaspoons fresh thyme, or
    1/2 teaspoon dried*
4 slices bacon
1/2 cup (1/4 pound) butter
Juice of 2 lemons
1 tablespoon Worcestershire sauce
2 teaspoons dry vermouth
1/2 cup finely chopped green onions
1/4 cup finely chopped parsley

Clean the fish well and remove the top and bottom fins, but leave the heads on.

Mix the salt, peppers, and herbs together in a small bowl and rub the mixture well all over the fish. Cut the bacon slices in half and wrap two halves around each fish, securing with toothpicks so that the fish will lie flat on either side. Preheat a broiler to highest heat. Oil a heavy black iron skillet well, pouring off any excess oil, and place it in the broiler for 15 minutes. Then place the fish in the skillet and return to the broiler. (If the skillet will only hold two fish comfortably, do two batches.) Cook the fish for 4 minutes, then turn them over carefully, trying to keep the skin intact, and broil for 4 minutes more. This method cooks the fish very quickly, on both sides at once, sealing in the juices and producing a delicious result.

Melt the butter in a small saucepan over medium heat and add the lemon juice, Worcestershire sauce, vermouth, green onions, and parsley. Let simmer for 3 minutes. Pour over the cooked fish and serve immediately.

Serves 4.

❦ SMOKED FISH ❦

Smoking fish is nothing new, but serving it hot will be a novelty to most people. Once you taste how the heat brings the flavors out, you'll be converted. And if you're lucky enough to have left-overs, you can make a terrific pasta with them.

4 fillets of fresh, firm saltwater
  fish, 10–12 ounces each
1 tablespoon salt
1 teaspoon ground red pepper
1 teaspoon ground black pepper
1 teaspoon ground white pepper
3 garlic cloves, chopped fine

1/2 cup (1/4 pound) butter
Juice of 2 lemons
1 tablespoon Worcestershire sauce
2 teaspoons dry vermouth
1/2 cup finely chopped green
  onions
1/4 cup finely chopped parsley

Pat the fillets dry. In a small bowl, mix together the salt and peppers and rub the mixture with the garlic all over the fish. Place the fillets in a smoker and smoke for 5 hours at low heat. (Follow the general instructions on smoking in Basics.) Be sure the heat is not too high, or the fish will dry out.

Ideally, you should serve the fish directly from the smoker. Just before it is done, melt the butter in a small saucepan over medium-high heat and add the lemon juice, Worcestershire sauce, vermouth, green onions, and parsley. Pour the sauce over the fish and serve immediately.

You can also smoke the fish in advance. Let it cool, then wrap it in plastic and place it in the refrigerator. When you are ready to serve, preheat the broiler to 400°F. Place the fillets on a cookie sheet or in a large flat pan. Prepare the butter sauce as above and pour it over. Place the pan under the broiler just long enough to heat the fish through, 3–4 minutes.

Serves 4.

🦐 SMOKED FISH WITH PASTA 🦐

2 cups heavy cream
3 teaspoons fresh basil, or
*   1 teaspoon dried*
3 teaspoons fresh thyme, or
*   1 teaspoon dried*
1 teaspoon salt
1/2 teaspoon ground red pepper
1/2 teaspoon ground black pepper
1/4 teaspoon ground white pepper

1/2 teaspoon minced fresh
*   garlic*
About 4 cups Smoked Fish
*   in small pieces*
1/4 cup chopped green onions
1/4 cup chopped parsley
1 pound angel hair pasta,
*   fresh if possible*
1/2 cup olive oil

Pour the cream into a large heavy skillet and place over medium-high heat. Bring it to a simmer, stirring often. Add the herbs and seasonings and let reduce until it is nice and thick—it should coat the spoon heavily (10–15 minutes). Add the smoked fish and the green onions and parsley and continue to cook for 2–3 minutes more.

Meanwhile, cook the pasta until not quite al dente in plenty of boiling salted water. Drain and mix with the olive oil and let stand a couple of minutes (the heat it retains will complete the cooking while the sauce is finishing). Divide the pasta among big preheated gumbo bowls, spoon the sauce equally over each serving, and serve immediately.

Serves 6.

❦ CAJUN SEAFOOD AU GRATIN ❧

This dish should really be prepared fresh. It doesn't take long to make, and your guests or family will enjoy watching you prepare it. You don't have to use all three kinds of seafood, either. Try it with just one or two of them, increasing the amounts, or substitute other kinds of seafood that are readily available.

1 pint heavy cream
1 tablespoon fresh basil, or
* 2 teaspoons dried*
1 tablespoon fresh thyme, or
* 2 teaspoons dried*
2 teaspoons salt
2 teaspoons ground black pepper
1½ teaspoons ground red
* pepper*
1 teaspoon ground white pepper
1 cup chopped green onions
1 cup chopped parsley

½ pound medium shrimp, peeled
* and deveined*
½ pound crawfish tails (see
* Sources)*
½ pound lump or white crab
* meat (we use blue crab)*
1½ cups grated cheese (Jack,
* Swiss, and American work*
* well)*
2 tablespoons grated Parmesan
* cheese*

Pour the cream into a large heavy skillet or saucepan and place over medium-high heat. The cream will rise before it begins to boil; just stir it to keep it from overflowing. Once it begins to simmer, add the herbs, salt, peppers, green onions, and parsley, and continue to let simmer until it becomes thick, 7–8 minutes. Stir in the shrimp and let cook 3–4 minutes, then add the crawfish. Mix well and let cook 2–3 minutes. Gently fold in the crab meat (you paid a premium price for it, so don't destroy those precious lumps). Let cook 2–3 minutes more, then add the 1½ cups cheese and stir gently until it has melted.

Preheat the broiler. Pour the hot seafood mixture into a large ovenproof dish or individual ramekins. Sprinkle the top with the Parmesan cheese and glaze under the broiler. Serve immediately.

Serves 6.

❧ SEAFOOD AU GRATIN ❧
IN EGGPLANT PIROGUES

3 medium eggplants
1½ tablespoons salt
2 teaspoons ground red pepper
1 teaspoon ground black
  pepper
1 teaspoon ground white
  pepper
2 eggs

12 ounces beer (not too dark), or
  1½ cups milk
2 cups all-purpose flour
Oil for deep-frying
1 recipe Cajun Seafood au
  Gratin (see preceding recipe)
2 tablespoons grated Parmesan
  cheese

Halve the eggplants lengthwise and scoop out the pulp, leaving a ½-inch shell. (Save the eggplant flesh for Cajun Eggplant Dressing, page 73.) Place the eggplant shells in a large bowl and cover with cold water.

In a small bowl, mix together the salt and peppers; set aside. In a medium mixing bowl, beat together the eggs and beer or milk and half the salt-pepper mixture. Place the flour in a large shallow pan and mix in the rest of the salt-pepper mixture.

Fill a Dutch oven or other large heavy pot with oil to a depth of about 5 inches and heat to 350°F. Drain the eggplant halves and dry them well. Dip them first in the egg batter, then in the flour mixture, coating them well. Shake off any excess flour. Fry the eggplant boats (pirogues) two at a time in the hot oil until they are golden brown all over, about 8 minutes. Drain on paper toweling.

Preheat the broiler. Place the pirogues on a cookie sheet or in a large flat pan. Divide the hot seafood mixture evenly among them, sprinkle with the Parmesan cheese, and place under the broiler for a couple of minutes to glaze them. Serve immediately.

Serves 6.

Poultry
and Game

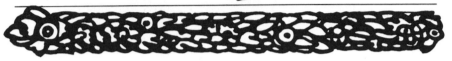

It's said that the difference between a Creole and a Cajun is that a Creole takes three chickens to feed one family, while a Cajun takes one chicken and feeds three families. As you cook your way through this chapter, you'll begin to see that there's more than a grain of truth to the story—which is not to say, however, that southwestern Louisiana is lacking in poultry and game. In fact, hunting is so much a part of Cajun culture that some wives say good-bye to their husbands in November and don't see them again until February. The season starts in September, with blue-wing teal and alligator. Next come rabbits and squirrel, followed by deer and migrant ducks and geese. Then it's on into winter, when woodcock and quail are abundant.

The hunting life revolves around the camps—not the fishing camps on the coast where the whole family goes for the weekend, but the hunting camps inland in the marshes. They're not so far away as the crow flies, but the land in our part of the country changes so rapidly that they seem to lie in another world altogether. They're a world apart in another way, too. Only the men go to the hunting camps, and there are still a few full-time trappers who subsist year-round on what they trap. But even the more typical weekend hunter doesn't just hunt while he's away at the camp. Cooking and eating are essential parts of the hunting life, too, and Cajun men are good cooks. Some of the most interesting techniques for cooking fresh game—sauce piquante, for example—come from camp recipes. In fact, having to feed a crew of hungry hunters out of one pot with no grocery store nearby is not bad training for a home cook with a family's worth of healthy appetites to satisfy.

There's another lesson to be learned from the hunter—he may have a general idea of what he'd like to eat for supper, but he has no way of knowing exactly what edible creatures he's going to run into in the course of the day. That's a good attitude to take with you to the grocery store. Try shopping with a general idea of the *style* in which you feel like cooking and eating, then see what's cheap, fresh, and plentiful, and plan your menu accordingly. You'll find yourself spending less and enjoying your meals more. Isn't that what's important?

Most of the recipes in this chapter work as well with chicken or domestic duck as they do with game, which can be difficult to come by. Rabbit has become very widely available recently, though, and even Louisiana alligator meat can be found in many parts of the country, so keep your eyes peeled. I also recommend that you make every attempt to locate a supplier of fresh, free-range poultry—in taste and texture, it's infinitely superior to any frozen bird. And don't overlook old hens and roosters, particularly if you can get fresh ones; the long, slow cooking called for in many of the recipes that follow produces a fork-tender, savory dish, even if it's no spring chicken you're fooling with.

❦ MAW MAW'S CHICKEN STEW ❧

When we were growing up, we used to go over to my mother's parents in Jeanerette for Sunday dinner. They owned a store in which they sold the chickens they raised and the eggs the chickens laid. On the way we'd always ask, "Mama, do you think Maw Maw's gonna have chicken stew?" and she'd answer, "Of course. She wouldn't have anything else."

1 hen, fresh if possible, about 5
   pounds
2 tablespoons salt
1 tablespoon ground red pepper
2 teaspoons ground black pepper
2 teaspoons ground white pepper
5 cups dark roux (see Basics)
3 large yellow onions,
   chopped fine

2 large bell peppers,
   chopped fine
2 celery ribs, chopped fine
2 quarts good chicken stock
   (see Basics)
2 cups sliced fresh mushrooms
2 cups chopped green
   onions
1 cup chopped parsley

Pull off the neck and back fat from the hen and reserve; cut the hen into small serving pieces. In a small bowl, mix together the salt and peppers. Season the chicken pieces well with about a third of this mixture.

In a large heavy skillet, preferably iron, render the chicken fat (if your skillet is not well seasoned, you may need to add a little oil). Add the chicken pieces and brown well on all sides over medium-high heat. Remove.

It's best to make the roux in the pan at this point, using the fat that remains in the pan as part of the oil. If you have made your roux ahead, add it to the skillet now and get it good and hot. Add half the onions, bell peppers, and celery to the hot roux, remove from the heat, and let cool, stirring occasionally.

Place the chicken stock in a heavy 6–8-quart stockpot, add the rest of the onions, bell peppers, and celery, and bring to a boil over high heat. Reduce the heat to medium and begin whisking or stirring in the roux, a cup at a time, making sure it dissolves completely before you add more, until you have a medium-thick stock (it should be a little heavier than a gumbo stock). Stir in the rest of the salt-pepper mixture and let simmer over low heat, stirring often, for 45 minutes to 1 hour. Add the chicken pieces and continue to simmer until the hen is tender, 1½–2 hours, depending on the toughness of the bird. Remove from heat and let stand 5–10 minutes, to allow the fat to rise to the top. Skim off and discard the fat and return the stew to a simmer over medium-high heat. Add the mushrooms, green onions, and parsley and let simmer 3–5 minutes more. Serve the chicken on plates with rice alongside and gravy over all.

Serves 5–6.

❧ CHICKEN PIE ❧

For those of you who like to bake, here's a wonderful, inexpensive supper dish. If you prepare the pastry in advance, you can assemble it in minutes.

1 recipe pastry from Crawfish Pie (page 62), omitting the sugar

3–4 cups cold leftover Chicken Stew (see preceding recipe; more gravy than chicken is fine)

Preheat the oven to 350°F. Roll out two thirds of the pastry to about ¼-inch thickness and line a 9-inch pie shell with it. Remove the chicken from the stew, debone it, and mix it back in. (If you have served Petit Pois with the stew, as we always do, add any of them that are left, too. Cooked carrots are also good.) Pour the stew into the pie shell.

Roll out the remaining pastry, cut it in strips, and arrange it in a lattice pattern on top. Pinch the lattice to the shell around the edges to hold it in place. Place the pie in the oven and bake it until it is golden brown and bubbling, about 35 minutes. Remove the pie and let it stand for a moment or two, then serve cut in wedges.

Serves 5–6.

❧ CHICKEN SPAGHETTI ☙

If you have leftover Chicken Stew but don't have time to make pastry, here's an even simpler way of getting a whole new meal out of it.

Debone the chicken from 3–4 cups of leftover stew, chop it, and return it to the stew. Bring it to a simmer over medium-high heat. Cook 1 pound of pasta just until al dente in plenty of boiling salted water. Drain it well and place it in a large bowl. Pour the stew over, mix well, and serve immediately.

Serves 4.

❧ CHICKEN SALAD ☙

Simple as it seems, this is a very old family favorite. What makes it special is the extra flavor that the chicken stock gives. We like to serve it as part of a buffet at receptions and family celebrations.

2 whole fryers, about 3 pounds
    each
3 carrots
2 onions
8 eggs
1/2 cup finely chopped bell pepper
1/4 cup finely chopped dill pickles
1/2 cup finely chopped olives

1 cup finely chopped celery
1 cup finely chopped green
    onions
1/2 cup finely chopped parsley
1 tablespoon salt
1 teaspoon ground red pepper
1 teaspoon ground black pepper
1 cup mayonnaise (see page 156)

Place the fryers in a large heavy stockpot and add the carrots, onions, and water to cover. Bring to a boil over medium-high heat and let simmer until the chickens are tender, 45 minutes or so.

Meanwhile, hard-boil the eggs, then immerse them in cold water to cool them quickly. Peel them and separate the whites from the yolks. Reserve the yolks, chop the whites, and reserve them also.

When the fryers are tender, remove them from the stock and let them cool. Cool the stock, too, then skim off the fat. Measure out ½ cup of stock and reserve the rest for another use. Bone and skin the chicken and cut it in 1-inch pieces (scissors work well for this). Place the chicken in a large mixing bowl, add the bell pepper, pickles, olives, celery, green onions, parsley, salt, peppers, and chopped egg whites and mix well. Mash the reserved yolks with 5 tablespoons of the chicken stock and 3 tablespoons of the mayonnaise; add to the chicken mixture and mix well. Then mix in the rest of the stock and mayonnaise. Cover and refrigerate for at least 3 hours. If you wish to mold the salad, pack it into the molds and refrigerate several hours or overnight. I like to serve it on a big platter garnished with some nice lettuce leaves and wedges of fresh tomato.

Serves 8–10.

DEEP-FRIED TURKEY

There's probably no place more hectic than the kitchen on Thanksgiving Day. With this recipe, you men—or women, for that matter—can earn brownie points by volunteering to prepare the main course *and* escape from the confusion to the outdoors. And you'll enjoy more than the nice crisp fall weather—deep-frying gives the turkey a wonderful crisp skin and keeps the delicate breast meat perfectly moist.

6 tablespoons salt

2 tablespoons ground red pepper

2 tablespoons ground black pepper

1 tablespoon ground white pepper

1 turkey, fresh if possible, about
   14 pounds

4 eggs

1 cup milk

12 ounces beer (not too
   dark)

8 cups all-purpose flour

Vegetable oil for deep-frying

In a small bowl, mix together the salt and peppers. Season the turkey well outside, under the skin, and in the cavity with a third of the mixture. Beat together the eggs, milk, and beer and another third of the salt-pepper mixture and pour slowly over the turkey to moisten it well all over. Mix together the flour and the remainder of the salt-pepper mixture, place it in a large shallow pan, and dredge the turkey well on all sides.

Half fill a large (10-gallon) heavy stockpot with oil and heat to 300°F over medium heat. (It's best to cook the turkey outside, if possible, using a butane burner. Wherever you do it, though, be very careful not to spill any of the hot oil, to avoid starting a fire.) Lower the turkey, breast side down, into the hot oil—slowly, so that the temperature of the oil doesn't drop too much. (A piece of fishing line attached to the turkey legs will help keep your hands from getting burnt.) Deep-fry the turkey, allowing 7 minutes a pound. (If the turkey will only float on its back initially, you'll need to turn it over three-quarters of the way through cooking.) Remove and let stand on paper toweling for about 10 minutes. Carve and serve as you would a roasted turkey, accompanied by the usual fixings.

Serves 10–12.

❧ RICE DRESSING ❧

This dressing and the Cornbread Dressing that follows are staple Cajun dishes. The amounts given make a lot. We like to freeze the dressing base in half-pint containers and defrost them as needed— a container of dressing base to 2 cups of raw rice or 3 cups crumbled cornbread, which is enough to feed six to eight people. The rice dressing is used mostly to accompany poultry (though I especially like it with barbecue, too); the cornbread dressing is typically served with pork, venison, and other rich meats. And, of course, they can be used to stuff turkeys and other fowl. But there's no hard and fast rule about when to serve either of them—just remember that no holiday meal is complete without at least one of them.

2 pounds chicken livers
1 pound chicken gizzards
1 pound pork liver
3 medium onions, chopped
2 medium bell peppers, chopped
3 celery ribs, chopped
3 garlic cloves
2 tablespoons vegetable oil
2 cups chicken stock (see Basics)

1 tablespoon dark roux (see Basics)
2 teaspoons salt
1 teaspoon ground red pepper
1 teaspoon ground black pepper
¹/₂ teaspoon ground white pepper
5–6 shots Tabasco sauce
4 cups raw rice
1 cup finely chopped green onions
1 cup finely chopped parsley

Using a food mill fitted with a medium disk or a food processor fitted with a steel blade, roughly grind together the chicken livers, gizzards, pork liver, onions, bell peppers, celery, and garlic. Place the oil in a Dutch oven or other large heavy pot and place over medium heat. Add the ground meat mixture and the chicken stock and cook, stirring occasionally, for about 1 hour. Stir in the roux and the seasonings and continue to cook over medium heat for 30 minutes more. This is your dressing base; you should have about a quart. (The dressing can be prepared in advance to this point and frozen, or stored in the refrigerator for up to a week.)

Meanwhile, boil or steam the rice according to the directions on the package. In a large bowl, mix together the hot dressing base and the cooked rice. Add the green onions and the parsley and toss well, being careful not to mash the rice. Serve hot.

CORNBREAD DRESSING

3 cups yellow cornmeal
3 tablespoons flour
2 teaspoons baking powder
2 teaspoons salt

3 eggs, beaten
2 cups milk
3 tablespoons vegetable
    oil

Preheat the oven to 350°F. Sift together the dry ingredients into a large mixing bowl and add the eggs, milk, and oil. Mix well. Pour the batter into a greased 9 × 13-inch baking pan and bake until firm and golden, 20–25 minutes. Remove and let cool.

Proceed as for Rice Dressing, substituting 6 cups crumbled cornbread for the rice. Place the finished mixture in a large greased baking pan or dish. The dressing should be very moist—if it is too dry, pour a little chicken stock on top. Bake at 325°F until the top is nicely browned, about 45 minutes.

❧ SMOTHERED QUAIL ❧

Smothering is a multipurpose Cajun technique that works wonders with everything from game to snap beans. It's similar to what the rest of the world knows as braising—the ingredients are briefly browned or sautéed, then cooked with a little liquid over low heat for a long time. The result is a tender, satisfying dish that makes its own gravy. Other game and poultry that work well this way are squirrel, rabbit, hen, and especially wild duck. (Probably a third of wild ducks caught in our neck of the woods find themselves made into gumbo; the rest wind up smothered.)

1 tablespoon salt
2 teaspoons ground red pepper
2 teaspoons ground black pepper
1 teaspoon ground white pepper
12 fresh quail
1½ cups all-purpose flour
½ cup vegetable oil

3 medium onions, chopped fine
2 medium bell peppers, chopped fine
1 celery rib, chopped fine
1 cup chicken stock (see Basics)
1 cup chopped green onions
½ cup chopped parsley

In a small bowl, mix together the salt and peppers. Season the quail inside and out with about half the mixture. Place the flour in a large flat pan and dredge the quail lightly on all sides. Place the oil in a Dutch oven or other large heavy pot over medium-high heat and brown the quail well on all sides. Remove the quail to a platter and discard all but 1 tablespoon of the oil. Add the onions, bell peppers, and celery, reduce the heat to low, and sauté for 2–3 minutes. Return the quail to the pot, stir well, and add the stock. Cover the pot and let cook over lowest possible heat until the quail are very tender, about 1½ hours. Stir once during cooking to be sure nothing is sticking to the pot. Remove from heat and let stand a few minutes to allow fat to rise to the top. Skim and discard the fat and stir in the green onions and parsley. Serve on individual plates, with rice alongside and gravy over all.

Serves 4–6.

Roux from light to
dark (*counterclockwise
from lower left*): peanut
butter, medium
and dark

Redfish Courtbouillon

Crawfish Bisque

A crawfish boil

Crawfish Yvonne

Fresh Louisiana seafood at Cypremort Point: oysters, redfish, shrimp, blue crabs

Lady Fish (*foreground*); Redfish Eugenie
(*background*)

Frogs' Legs with Jambalaya

A pirogue on the bayou with a cargo of ducks and rabbits

(*Opposite*) Pasta with Crawfish and Tasso

Smothered Sausage with Cajun Hash Browns

Chicken and Sausage Gumbo

Rabbit Sauce Piquante

Roast Leg of Pork with Cajun Rice Dressing, Maque Choux, and Cornbread

Sweets (*clockwise from left*): Bread Pudding, Pecan Pie, strawberries and cream, Pineapple Upside-Down Cake

The Patouts—Andre, Gigi, Gene, Alex, Ms. Ann, Liz, Mitch, and Mo Mo (*seated*)—and the bounty of Louisiana

❧ RABBIT SPAGHETTI ☙

If you look beyond the rabbits, you'll find that this is a good basic spaghetti sauce. As with so many of our recipes, it lets you be creative and turn what's available to advantage, from meatballs or chicken to venison, turtle, or alligator.

2 rabbits, fresh if possible, about
    4 pounds each
1½ tablespoons salt
2 teaspoons ground red pepper
2 teaspoons ground black pepper
1 teaspoon ground white pepper
1 tablespoon fresh basil, or
    1 teaspoon dried
1 tablespoon fresh thyme, or
    1 teaspoon dried
1 tablespoon fresh oregano, or
    1 teaspoon dried
All-purpose flour for dredging
2 cups olive oil

2 medium onions, chopped fine
2 medium bell peppers,
    chopped fine
2 celery ribs, chopped fine
4 garlic cloves, minced
5–6 large fresh tomatoes, peeled,
    seeded, and roughly chopped
1 can (4 ounce) tomato paste
1 teaspoon sugar
1 pound fresh mushrooms, sliced
1½ pounds spaghetti, fresh if
    possible
1 cup chopped green onions
1 cup chopped parsley

Cut the rabbits into serving pieces. In a small bowl, mix together the salt and peppers (and the herbs, if you are using dried ones). Place the flour in a large shallow pan with one quarter of the seasonings and dredge the rabbit pieces lightly on all sides. Pour the olive oil into a Dutch oven or other large heavy pot and place over medium-high heat. Add the rabbit pieces and brown on all sides, then remove them to a platter. Add the onions, bell peppers, celery, and garlic and sauté over medium-high heat, stirring occasionally, until they are tender, 15–20 minutes. Stir in the tomatoes, tomato paste, sugar, and the rest of the salt-pepper-herb mixture (add all the herbs now if you are using fresh ones). Reduce the heat to low and let simmer about 2 hours, stirring occasionally. If the sauce begins to scorch, stir in a little water. Add the rabbit pieces and continue to cook until the meat is very tender, 1½ to 2 hours. Add the mushrooms and cook for 15 to 20 minutes more.

Cook the pasta just until al dente in plenty of boiling salted water. Drain it well. (I like to mix it with a little olive oil.) Stir the green onions and parsley into the rabbit sauce, remove from heat, and serve over the pasta in individual bowls, with Parmesan cheese for sprinkling.

Serves 8–10.

❦ ALLIGATOR SAUCE PIQUANTE ❦

Sauce piquante, with its classic combination of roux and fresh tomatoes, is one of the oldest Cajun recipes. In fact, if you think of it more as a technique than as a recipe, you'll see that it's a great way to prepare all kinds of meat, poultry, and game—try it with turtle, frogs' legs, squirrel, rabbit, or plain old chicken (it's a perfect way to deal with a tough old rooster). Let the tenderness of the meat be your guide to cooking time.

4 pounds alligator bones
2 quarts water
3 pounds alligator meat
1 tablespoon salt
1 tablespoon ground red pepper
2 teaspoons ground black pepper
2 teaspoons ground white pepper
½ cup flour
¾ cup oil
3 cups medium roux (see Basics)

3 medium yellow onions, chopped coarse
2 medium bell peppers, chopped coarse
8–10 large tomatoes, peeled, seeded, and roughly chopped
6–8 shots Tabasco sauce
2 cups chopped green onions
2 cups chopped parsley

Place the alligator bones and the water in a large stockpot and bring to a boil over medium-high heat. Reduce the heat and let boil slowly for 45 minutes to 1 hour. Remove the bones and skim and reserve the stock.

Cut the alligator meat into pieces about 1 by 2 inches. In a small bowl, mix together the salt and peppers. Season the alligator meat with about a third of this mixture and dredge it lightly in the flour. Place the oil in a Dutch oven or other large heavy pot and place over high heat. Add the alligator meat and brown well on all sides. Remove.

If you haven't made your roux in advance, make it in the pot at this point, adding oil to what remains in the pan to obtain the right amount. If your roux is already made, add it to the pot and get it good and hot. Remove the roux from the heat and stir in half each of the yellow onions and bell peppers. Let cool.

Add the tomatoes to the cooled roux mixture, place the pot over medium-high heat, and cook for 30 minutes, stirring often. Stir in the alligator stock, the remaining onions and bell peppers, the rest of the salt and pepper mixture, and the Tabasco sauce. Continue to cook over medium heat, stirring often, 45 minutes to 1 hour. Add the alligator meat and let simmer 30 minutes more until the meat is very tender. Stir in the green onions and parsley, remove from heat, and serve in gumbo bowls over rice.

Serves 6.

❧ FROGS' LEGS ❧

We get perfect, tender fresh frogs' legs in the spring and early fall. If you must, you can use frozen frogs' legs, but fresh ones are beyond compare.

Oil for deep-frying
2 cups beer (not too dark)
2 cups milk
4 eggs
¹/₂ cup flour
2 teaspoons salt

1 teaspoon ground red pepper
1 teaspoon ground black pepper
1 teaspoon ground white
 pepper
12–16 pairs frogs' legs (see
 Sources)

In a deep-fryer or other large heavy pot, pour oil to a depth of at least 3 inches. Place over high heat and heat to 375°F. Set a fry basket in the oil.

In a large mixing bowl, whisk together the beer, milk, eggs, flour, and seasonings until smooth. Dip the frogs' legs in the batter, pair by pair, holding them up to let the excess batter run off. Transfer them to the fry basket, holding on to them for a few seconds to keep them from sticking to the basket. Don't overcrowd the fryer—you will probably need to make two or three batches. Fry the frogs' legs until golden brown, 3–4 minutes. Remove and drain on paper toweling. Serve hot, with lemon wedges or Tartar Sauce (see page 90).

Serves 4–6.

❧ CHICKEN AND SAUSAGE JAMBALAYA ❧

Typically, jambalaya is made from leftovers, which become a savory base into which rice is mixed to get an entirely new meal. Shrimp Creole, Maw Maw's Chicken Stew, and smothered meat, poultry, and game all work wonderfully this way. This recipe will show you how to make jambalaya from scratch; once you get the idea, you can take it from there.

1 fryer, fresh if possible, 3–4 pounds
1½ tablespoons salt
3 teaspoons ground red pepper
2 teaspoons ground black pepper
2 teaspoons ground white pepper
1 pound smoked pork sausage, sliced ½ inch thick
2 large yellow onions, chopped fine
2 medium bell peppers, chopped fine

3 celery ribs, chopped fine
2 teaspoons chopped fresh basil, or ½ teaspoon dried
2 teaspoons fresh thyme, or ½ teaspoon dried
4–5 tablespoons dark roux (see Basics)
1 pint chicken stock (see Basics)
5–6 shots Tabasco sauce
2 cups raw rice
1 cup chopped green onions
1 cup chopped parsley

Cut the fryer into small serving pieces. In a small bowl, mix together the salt and peppers. Season the chicken with half this mixture. Place a Dutch oven or other large heavy pot over medium heat, add the sausage, and brown on all sides. Remove. Add the chicken to the pan, brown on all sides, and remove. Pour off any excess fat.

Reduce the heat, add the onions, bell peppers and celery, and sauté for 20 minutes, stirring occasionally. Stir in the herbs and the rest of the salt-pepper mixture and sauté for a few minutes more. Stir in the roux and let cook for a few minutes, to get it good and hot. Then slowly add the chicken stock until the mixture is a little thicker than a gumbo but not as thick as a stew. Stir in the Tabasco and let the mixture simmer slowly for 20 minutes, stirring often. Then add the sausage and chicken, cover, and cook over low heat until the chicken is very tender, stirring occasionally. A young fryer will take 45 minutes to an hour; an older fryer or roasting chicken may take longer.

Meanwhile, steam the rice (see Basics). When the chicken is tender, remove it to a serving platter. Transfer the rice to a large mixing bowl, and gradually add the jambalaya base until you get the consistency you like. (You will probably not use all the jambalaya base for this quantity of rice. Store the excess in the refrigerator for 3–4 days or freeze it.) Add the green onions and parsley and mix well. Serve on plates with the chicken alongside. (You can also bone the chicken and return it to the jambalaya base before mixing with the rice, but I prefer to serve it separately so that everyone can pick the part he likes.

Serves 6–8.

Meats

The *boucherie* is a Cajun tradition that dates back well over two hundred years. About once a month during slaughtering season—October to March—all the neighbors in the area would gather to slaughter a pig. The men would do the butchering and cleaning, and the women would prepare the boudin, tasso, sausage, and other delicacies. Not only was this an efficient way to process every part of the pig, it was also an occasion for neighboring families to get together and celebrate. And even though the boucherie has all but vanished today, many Cajun specialties derive from it—tasso, boudin, sausage, hogshead cheese, and so on. In fact, a number of the recipes in this chapter derive from that event. The boucherie lasted all day long, and dinner that day was typically a smothered backbone stew. Smothered pork chops are a good modern-day approximation of that dish. And the sausage, tasso, and other meat by-products prepared that day extended far beyond the season, and show up far beyond the scope of this chapter—in soups, stews, gumbos, and the like. After everyone had feasted at supper at sunset, it was time for the players and dancers, who closed out the evening with a grand *fey-do-do*—which in plain English means time for little children to go to sleep. You'll sleep well, too, after you've made a meal of smothered round steak or some other slow-cooked dish that's proved to you the wealth of flavor Cajun cooking can coax out of even an inexpensive cut of meat.

A few of the recipes in this chapter offer an almost complete contrast to these old-fashioned delicacies. Our award-winning Veal on the Teche, Lamb Boudreaux, and Tournedos Patout are superlative examples of the new Louisiana cooking. They combine time-honored cooking techniques—smoking and cream reductions, for example—in ways my ancestors never dreamed of, with results you'll be proud to serve at your fanciest dinner parties. And they show their origins in Cajun home-style cooking in another important way—they're just as easy to prepare in your kitchen.

So try Louisiana meat cooking, old style and new. I guarantee you'll discover adventures in eating in both directions.

❦ JAMBALAYA LAFITTE ❦

This wonderful jambalaya comes from my grandmother, Mo Mo. It can certainly stand on its own, but it also makes a wonderful side dish to accompany Redfish Eugenie, Lady Fish, Trout Michel, or Soft-Shell Crabs Elizabeth.

1 pound medium fresh shrimp,
  heads off
1½ cups diced cooked ham or
  tasso
1 tablespoon all-purpose flour
1 tablespoon vegetable oil
1 garlic clove, crushed
1 cup raw rice
1¼ cup chopped green onions
½ pound smoked sausage, sliced
  ½ inch thick
1 medium onion, chopped fine
1 celery rib, chopped fine
1 medium green pepper,
  chopped fine

2 medium tomatoes, peeled,
  seeded, and roughly chopped
1 bay leaf
2 teaspoons fresh thyme, or
  ½ teaspoon dried
2 teaspoons salt
1 teaspoon ground black pepper
½ teaspoon ground white pepper
1 teaspoon ground red pepper
1 cup dry white wine
1 dozen unwashed fresh shucked
  oysters
¼ cup chopped parsley

Remove the heads from the shrimp and peel and devein them. Place the heads and peels in a small saucepan, cover with water, and bring to a boil. Let simmer for about 20 minutes, then strain.

Dust the ham with the flour. Heat the oil in a Dutch oven or other large heavy pot over medium-high heat, add the ham and garlic, and brown on all sides. Remove. Add the rice and ¾ cup of the green onions and sauté, stirring frequently, until the rice is golden brown. Stir in the ham and garlic and the sausage, onion, celery, green pepper, tomatoes, bay leaf, thyme, salt, pepper, wine, and 1 cup of the shrimp stock; bring to a boil. Reduce heat, cover, and let simmer for about 20 minutes.

Add the shrimp, oysters, remainder of the green onions, and parsley to the rice mixture. Stir well, cover and let cook about 15 minutes more. Serve immediately, on flat plates.

Serves 6.

❦ BOUDIN ❧

Tourists coming through southern Louisiana are forever asking, "What is that stuff, b-o-u-d-i-n, I see advertised in front of gas stations, convenience stores, drugstores, and everywhere else?" The answer is, a wonderful Cajun fast food—a kind of sausage, really—that's definitely worth learning to make at home.

3 pounds boneless pork (Boston butt or shoulder), in large chunks
1 pound pork liver
3 cups raw rice
4 medium yellow onions, peeled and quartered

2 bunches green onions, chopped
2 tablespoons salt
2 teaspoons ground red pepper
1 tablespoon ground black pepper
2 teaspoons ground white pepper

Place the pork and pork liver in separate saucepans, cover with water, and bring to a boil. Skim, then reduce heat and simmer until tender, about 1 hour. Steam the rice (see Basics).

Remove the cooked pork and pork liver and let cool. Discard the liver stock. Reserve 1 pint of the pork stock and discard the rest. Put the pork, pork liver, and onions through a meat grinder fitted with a medium disk, or grind it coarse in a food processor. Transfer the mixture to a large bowl and mix in the green onions, salt, peppers, and cooked rice. (It will be easier to get a smooth mixture if you do this in batches.) Correct seasonings.

The boudin can be served as is, like Cajun Rice Dressing, to accompany meats or poultry. And the boudin base—everything except the rice—can be prepared in advance and stored in the refrigerator for a day or two, or frozen, until needed; when you are ready to serve, simply heat the base, cook the rice, and mix.

For traditional boudin, you can stuff the finished mixture into sausage casings. Put the finished sausages into a saucepan, add a little water, cover, and place over medium heat for a few minutes until the boudin is heated through.

Serves 10.

❦ TASSO ❧

This is probably the first dish you should try once you've mastered the basics of smoking (see Basics). Tasso is a unique Cajun product, not so much a dish in itself as a tremendously flavorful delicacy that will transform beans, soups, jambalaya—even sophisticated pasta sauces and crawfish dishes. And you can tell your guests proudly, "That's *my* tasso."

8–10 pounds boneless pork butt
5 tablespoons salt
5 tablespoons ground red pepper
3 tablespoons ground black
  pepper

3 tablespoons ground white pepper
2 tablespoons paprika
2 tablespoons cinnamon
2 tablespoons garlic powder or
  granulated garlic

Trim the pork of all excess fat and cut it into strips about 1 inch thick and at least 4 inches long. Mix together the seasonings and place in a shallow pan. Roll each strip of pork in the seasoning mixture and place on a tray. Cover with plastic and refrigerate for several hours (if you have time, let it sit for a day or two). Prepare a smoker as directed in Basics. Place the pork strips on a grill or rod and smoke until done, 5–7 hours. Don't let the smoker get too hot. Remove the meat and let cool completely. Then wrap well in foil and plastic. The tasso will keep well in the refrigerator for up to 10 days; it also freezes well.

ᜊ PURE PORK SAUSAGE ᜆ

If you've always wanted to make your own sausage, here's a wonderful, easy recipe for pure pork sausage to try. You can fry it for breakfast or supper as you would any sausage, use it in gumbos and jambalayas, or smoke it.

10 pounds pork butt
¹/₄ cup salt
2 tablespoons ground black pepper

2 tablespoons ground red pepper
1 tablespoon ground white pepper

Bone the pork butts and cut the meat into chunks. Place the bones in a large stockpot, cover with water, and bring to a boil. Skim, reduce heat slightly, and let simmer for an hour or two. Coarsely grind the pork in a meat grinder or food processor. Transfer it to a bowl and thoroughly mix in the salt and peppers. Add enough of the pork stock to make a very moist mixture (about a quart). Stuff into sausage casings. You can also roll the sausage mixture into cylinders, about an inch in diameter, wrap them in foil, and chill overnight. Cut into lengths and use as you would any sausage. The uncooked sausage will keep in the refrigerator for 3–4 days; it also freezes well.

Makes 7–8 pounds sausage.

❦ SMOTHERED SAUSAGE ❦

This dish is a classic example of the virtues of Cajun smothering. The quick browning and long slow cooking of the sausage with onions, bell peppers, and celery turn sausage into a dish you can be proud to serve to family and friends, any time of day.

2 pounds pure pork or other fresh
   sausage
2 medium yellow onions,
   chopped fine
2 medium bell peppers,
   chopped fine
3 celery ribs, chopped fine

½ teaspoon salt
¼ teaspoon ground black pepper
¼ teaspoon ground red pepper
¼ teaspoon ground white pepper
1 tablespoon dark roux (optional)
½ cup chopped green onions
½ cup chopped parsley

Place the sausage in a large heavy skillet with a close-fitting lid. Add water to cover and bring to a boil over medium-high heat. Let cook, uncovered, until all the water evaporates. Continue cooking, turning the sausage so that they brown well on all sides and don't stick. Pour off any excess fat. Add the onions, bell peppers, celery, salt and peppers, and an additional 1 cup water. Stir well, scraping the bottom of the pan to loosen any bits of sausage that may have stuck. Reduce heat, cover, and let cook for 45 minutes to 1 hour. Remove the sausages and let the pan juices sit for 5–10 minutes to allow any grease to rise to the top. Skim and discard the grease. If you like a thicker gravy, stir in the roux and let simmer 20 minutes more. Add the sausage along with the green onions and parsley and let simmer, uncovered, 3–4 minutes more. Serve immediately. This is wonderful with grits for breakfast or brunch, or with Cajun Hash Brown Potatoes or White Beans and Rice for supper.

Serves 4–6.

☙ SMOTHERED ROUND STEAK ❧

Here is a basic recipe for smothered meat. It will allow you to get a tender, flavorful dish that makes its own gravy from even an inexpensive cut of meat. Try it with cube or flank steaks, round or chuck roasts, short ribs, pork or veal chops.

1 round steak, about 2 pounds	*¹/₂ cup vegetable oil*
2 teaspoons salt	*3 medium onions, chopped*
¹/₂ teaspoon ground black pepper	*2 bell peppers, chopped*
1 teaspoon ground red pepper	*1 celery rib, chopped*
1 teaspoon ground white pepper	*1 cup beef stock or*
All-purpose flour for dredging	* water*

Season the roast with one half of the salt and peppers. Dust with flour on all sides. Heat the oil in a Dutch oven or other large heavy pot over medium-high heat, add the steak, and brown well on all sides. Remove the meat and pour off all but 1 teaspoon of the oil. Add half the onions, bell peppers, celery, the other half of the seasonings, and the stock or water. Stir well and reduce the heat to the lowest possible point. Return the roast to the pot and cover with the remaining vegetables. Cover and let cook until the meat is very tender, about 1 hour and 15 minutes.

Serve the meat in slices, with rice alongside and gravy over all.

When you try this recipe with other kinds of meat, be sure to adjust the cooking times accordingly—let tenderness be your guide. For extra flavorful roasts, try larding with slivers of garlic before smothering.

Serves 4–6.

❧ BOSTON BUTT PORK ROAST ❧

This is a basic roasting technique that works equally well with fresh pork ham or loin, leg, or shoulder of lamb or veal, beef sirloin tip or rib roast, or just about any other kind of roast you can think of. Try it for next Sunday's dinner and see for yourself.

1 Boston butt pork roast, 5–6
  pounds
3 garlic cloves
1 tablespoon salt
2 teaspoons ground red pepper
1½ teaspoons ground black
  pepper
1 teaspoon ground white pepper

2 medium onions, chopped fine
1 medium bell pepper,
  chopped fine
2 cups water
1 tablespoon dark roux (see
  Basics)
½ cup chopped green onions
½ cup chopped parsley

Trim the roast of any excess fat. Mince the garlic very fine and combine it with the salt and peppers in a small bowl. Make 5 or 6 incisions in the roast and stuff some of this mixture into them. Rub the remainder on the surface of the roast, wrap well in plastic, and place in the refrigerator several hours or overnight.

Preheat the oven to 250°F. Transfer the roast to a pan or roaster, cover with the onions and bell pepper, and add the water. Cook uncovered in the oven until the meat reaches 165°F on a meat thermometer, 5–7 hours (it should be not at all pink inside, but still juicy.) If you want to speed up the cooking process, you can cook the roast at 350°F, which will take 3–4 hours, but the longer, slower cooking will give a more tender and flavorful result.

Transfer the roast to a serving platter and pour the pan juices into a saucepan, being sure to scrape loose any particles that have stuck to the bottom of the pan. Let stand for 15 minutes, then skim the grease from the top and discard. Bring the gravy to a simmer over medium-high heat, then reduce the heat and stir in the roux, being sure it dissolves completely. Let simmer for 15 minutes; if it becomes too thick, add a little water. Stir in the green onions and parsley and remove from heat. Serve the sliced roast with rice alongside and gravy over all. For a special treat, try it with Cajun Rice Dressing (page 110) or Boudin (page 124).

Serves 6–8.

❧ TOURNEDOS PATOUT ❧

This is a great example of the new hybrid Louisiana cooking. It takes advantage of the subtle flavor smoking produces and marries it with a creamy crawfish sauce and fried eggplant. If you can't smoke the tenderloin, or don't want to, simply slice it into 1-inch fillets and grill them over charcoal.

*1 whole tenderloin of beef, about
    4 pounds
3 tablespoons salt
1 tablespoon ground red pepper
1 tablespoon ground black pepper
2 teaspoons ground white pepper
1 pint heavy cream
1 tablespoon chopped fresh basil,
    or 1 teaspoon dried
1 tablespoon fresh thyme, or
    1 teaspoon dried
Dash of nutmeg*

*¹/₂ cup chopped green onions
¹/₂ cup chopped parsley
1 pound peeled crawfish tails
    (see Sources)
Vegetable oil for deep-frying
2 eggplants, long, skinny ones
    if possible
3 eggs
2 cups milk
2 cups all-purpose flour for
    dredging*

Prepare a smoker as directed in Basics. Remove the silvery membrane surrounding the tenderloin. In a small bowl, mix together the salt and peppers. Season the meat heavily with this mixture—you'll need about 2 tablespoons of it. Place the meat on the smoker and smoke until it registers rare on a meat thermometer, 6–8 hours.

Pour the cream into a large heavy skillet and place over medium-high heat. Bring to a boil, stirring often, and add the basil, thyme, 1 tablespoon of the salt-pepper mixture, the nutmeg, green onions, and parsley. Continue to simmer until the cream thickens; it should fall from the spoon in heavy drops, and the last drop should cling to the spoon. Add the crawfish tails. The liquid in them will thin out the sauce, so continue to simmer until the sauce regains a thick consistency.

Meanwhile, pour oil into a Dutch oven or other large heavy pot to a depth of at least 3 inches and heat to 350°F over medium-high heat. Peel the eggplants and slice them crosswise into ¾-inch rounds. Sprinkle with ½ tablespoon of the salt-pepper mixture. Beat together the eggs, milk, and 1 tablespoon of the salt-pepper mixture. Combine the flour with the remaining tablespoon of the salt-pepper mixture and place it in a shallow pan. Dip the eggplant slices in the egg batter, dredge lightly in the flour to coat on all sides, and deep-fry until golden brown on both sides, about 3 minutes. Be careful not to crowd the pot—you may need to fry in batches. Drain the eggplant slices on paper toweling.

Remove the tenderloin from the smoker and slice ½ inch thick. (You can also smoke the tenderloin in advance and rewarm the slices quickly in a skillet with a little butter.) To serve, place 2 slices of eggplant on each plate, top each slice with a slice of tenderloin, and cover with the crawfish sauce.

Serves 8.

❧ LAMB BOUDREAUX ❧

This wonderful lamb dish won a gold medal at the 1984 Acadiana Culinary Classic. It's another golden example of the new Louisiana cooking. If you have some of the crawfish sauce left over, don't fret—use it tomorrow with pasta.

1 rack of lamb (or 2 pounds lamb medallions from a rack)
1 tablespoon salt
1 teaspoon ground red pepper
1 teaspoon ground black pepper
1 teaspoon ground white pepper
1 pint heavy cream

2 teaspoons chopped fresh basil, or ¹/₂ teaspoon dried
2 teaspoons fresh thyme, or ¹/₂ teaspoon dried
1¹/₂ cups diced tasso
1 pound peeled fresh crawfish tails (see Sources)
1 cup chopped green onions
1 cup chopped parsley

Debone the lamb and cut it into 8 medallions, about 1 inch thick. Mix together the salt and peppers and sprinkle the medallions on both sides with about a third of the mixture.

Pour the cream into a large heavy skillet and place over medium heat. Bring to a simmer and stir in the rest of the salt-pepper mixture and the herbs and tasso. Let reduce, stirring often, until the sauce is thick—it should fall from a spoon in large, heavy drops, and the last drop should cling to the spoon.

Meanwhile, preheat a charcoal or gas grill. Cook the lamb medallions to the desired degree of doneness (I like mine medium-rare). You can also broil them under high heat, turning once, or sauté them in a skillet over high heat in a little margarine or vegetable oil.

Add the crawfish tails, green onions, and parsley to the reduced cream sauce. The liquid from the crawfish tails will thin out the sauce, so let simmer until it regains a thick consistency, stirring frequently.

To serve, place two lamb medallions on each plate and top with the crawfish sauce.

Serves 4.

❦ VEAL ON THE TÈCHE ❧

Here's another Acadiana Culinary Classic gold medal winner. This is perhaps the easiest of our meat dishes with cream sauces, so you may want to try it first, before you move on to Lamb Boudreaux and Tournedos Patout.

12 veal scallops, 2–3 ounces
each
2 teaspoons salt
1 teaspoon ground red pepper
½ teaspoon ground black pepper
½ teaspoon ground white
pepper
1 pint heavy cream
½ cup chopped green onions
½ cup chopped parsley

1 tablespoon chopped fresh basil,
or 1 teaspoon dried
1 tablespoon fresh thyme, or
1 teaspoon dried
Dash of nutmeg
1 pound peeled crawfish tails (see
Sources)
1 cup all-purpose flour for
dredging
1 cup (½ pound) margarine

Pat the veal dry. In a small bowl, mix together the salt and peppers. Sprinkle the veal with about a third of this mixture on both sides and set aside.

Pour the cream into a large heavy skillet and place over medium-high heat. Bring it to a simmer and stir in the green onions, parsley, basil, thyme, nutmeg, and the rest of the salt-pepper mixture. Let the sauce reduce until the cream thickens; it should fall from the spoon in large heavy drops, and the last drop should cling to the spoon. Stir in the crawfish tails. The liquid in them will thin out the sauce considerably, so continue to let it simmer until it regains a thick consistency.

Dredge the veal lightly with flour on both sides. Heat the margarine in a large heavy skillet over medium-high heat. Add the veal and sauté, turning once, until golden brown, about 2 minutes on each side.

To serve, place two scallops on each plate and top with a generous amount of the crawfish sauce, dividing the crawfish tails evenly.

Serves 6.

❧ CABBAGE ROLLS ☙

Here's stuffed cabbage with a spicy twist—surprisingly enough, a traditional Cajun dish.

1 large head white cabbage	½ cup chopped green onions
1 pound ground beef	½ cup chopped parsley
1 teaspoon salt	2 cups raw rice
1 teaspoon ground red pepper	2 cans (8 ounce) Ro-tel tomatoes
1 teaspoon ground black pepper	2 cans (16 ounce) tomato
½ teaspoon ground white pepper	sauce
4 garlic cloves, minced	1 cup water

Bring a large kettle of water to a boil. Core the cabbage and place it in the boiling water base-side down. Remove each cabbage leaf as it comes loose and reserve.

In a large bowl, mix together the ground beef, salt, peppers, garlic, green onions, and parsley. Add the rice and mix well. Form the mixture into cylinders about 2 inches long and 1 inch in diameter. Roll each cylinder in a cabbage leaf, tucking in the ends to seal the stuffing completely.

Line the bottom of a Dutch oven or other large heavy pot with a layer of the remaining cabbage leaves. Layer the cabbage rolls on top. Drain the tomatoes and place them in a large mixing bowl. Break them up with your fingers and stir in the tomato sauce and the water. Pour the tomato mixture over the cabbage rolls and cover with another layer of cabbage leaves. Bring to a simmer over medium-high heat, then reduce the heat to low, cover, and let cook for about 1 hour and 45 minutes. Check occasionally to be sure there is sufficient liquid in the pot. If not, add a little water. Serve 4–6 rolls per person, with the sauce spooned over.

Serves 4–6.

❦ EGGPLANT CASSEROLE ❧

When you're in the mood for something different to serve with meat or poultry, try this casserole. Even if you've tried eggplant and vowed you'd never repeat the experience, give it one more chance with this dish. I especially like it with Smothered Round Steak, Maw Maw's Cajun Chicken Stew, or roast turkey. You can prepare it in advance and refrigerate or freeze it until cooking time, and you can also substitute mirlitons for the eggplant.

3 medium eggplants
1 tablespoon plus
  2 teaspoons salt
½ pound ground beef
2 medium onions, chopped
1 small bell pepper, chopped
1 celery rib, chopped

1 garlic clove, minced
1 tablespoon fresh thyme, or
  1 teaspoon dried
1 teaspoon ground red pepper
1 teaspoon ground black pepper
½ teaspoon ground white pepper
2 cups bread crumbs

Peel the eggplants and cut them into large cubes. Place the cubes in a large saucepan and sprinkle them with 1 tablespoon of the salt. Add 2 cups water and bring to a simmer over medium-high heat. Reduce the heat to low, cover, and let cook until the eggplant is soft, about 45 minutes. Drain off the water and mash the eggplant well with a potato masher, or puree in a food processor or blender.

Preheat the oven to 300°F. Brown the ground beef in a large heavy skillet over medium-high heat. Pour off the excess fat. Add the onions, bell pepper, celery, and garlic. Stir well, cover, and let cook until the vegetables are transparent, about 20 minutes. Stir in the thyme, the rest of the salt and the peppers, and cook for 5–7 minutes more. Mix in the pureed eggplant, cook 2 minutes more, and remove from heat. Stir in 1¾ cups of the bread crumbs.

Butter a casserole dish and sprinkle with the remaining bread crumbs. Pour in the eggplant mixture and bake in the oven until bubbling and just beginning to brown, about 20 minutes. Serve as a side dish to accompany poultry or meat.

Serves 8 as a side dish.

❧ GRILLADES ❧

A justly famous traditional Louisiana brunch dish.

2 pounds round of veal or beef
1 tablespoon salt
2 teaspoons ground red pepper
1 teaspoon ground black pepper
1 teaspoon ground white
  pepper
3 tablespoons all-purpose flour
1 cup vegetable oil
2 medium onions, chopped

1 large bell pepper, chopped
2 celery ribs, chopped
2 garlic cloves, minced
4 medium tomatoes, peeled,
  seeded, and roughly chopped
  (optional)
5 shots Tabasco sauce
1/4 cup red wine
1 cup beef stock or water

Cut the meat into rough squares, about 1 inch thick and 4 inches square. In a small bowl, mix together the salt and peppers. Sprinkle the meat with half of this mixture on all sides and sprinkle with flour. Pound the meat with a mallet to work in the flour. Pour the oil into a large heavy skillet or Dutch oven and place over high heat. Add the meat and brown well on both sides (you will probably need to do this in batches). Remove the meat to a platter and pour off all but 3 tablespoons of the oil from the pan.

Add the onions, bell pepper, celery, garlic, tomatoes, the rest of the salt-pepper mixture, and the Tabasco sauce to the pot and sauté over medium heat for about 15 minutes. Return the meat to the pot, stir in the wine and stock or water, cover, and simmer over medium-low heat until the meat is very tender, about 1½ hours.

Serve with buttered yellow grits or Cajun Hash Brown Potatoes.

Serves 4–6.

❦ CAJUN HOT TAMALES ❧

When I asked Mama for her hot tamale recipe she told me that it was not a Cajun dish. But I told her that it had been such a part of our household over the past thirty-odd years that we had to include it in the book. In fact, the very mention of hot tamales makes everyone in the family from ninety-year-old Mo Mo on down to the two-year-olds start jumping for joy.

Although this dish takes time, the ingredients are very simple. The only thing that you may have trouble obtaining is the parchment for the husks. We get ours in packages of one thousand from a local paper company that sells various household and commercial paper products, and they last a long time.

The meat mixture can be made in advance and frozen. Buy some beef chuck, pork butt, and soup bones when you spot a meat special in the supermarket, make a batch of tamale stuffing, and freeze it. Then one rainy day invite a few friends over, pull it out of the freezer, and have a tamale-rolling party. Your friends will have fun and will enjoy eating what they make.

Stock

6 pounds beef (round is good)	4 jalapeño peppers
4 pounds boneless pork	2 large potatoes, peeled
6 pounds beef bones	8 garlic cloves
6 large onions, peeled	1/2 cup salt
4 celery ribs	1/8 cup ground black pepper
	1/4 cup ground red pepper

Place the beef, pork, and beef bones in a large stockpot and cover with water. Bring to a boil over high heat, reduce heat to medium, skim, and let simmer for 1½ hours. Add the onions, celery, jalapeños, potatoes, garlic, and seasonings. Return to a boil and simmer for 45 minutes more. Strain, reserving the stock. Discard the bones and let the meat and vegetables cool. Put them through a meat grinder fitted with a medium disk or grind course in a food processor. Transfer the mixture to a large bowl and mix in:

⅓ cup salt	*5 ounces chili powder*
3 teaspoons ground cumin	*2 cans (12 ounce) paprika*
2 tablespoons ground red pepper	

Taste the mixture and correct the seasonings. The tamale stuffing may be prepared in advance to this point and stored in the refrigerator for 3 or 4 days or frozen.

Mush

4 pounds (12 cups) yellow	*¾ cup chili powder*
* cornmeal*	*¼ cup paprika*
4 tablespoons salt	*⅓ cup ground red pepper*

Place 2 quarts of the reserved stock and 1½ quarts of water in a large saucepan and bring to a boil. Mix the cornmeal, salt, chili powder, paprika, and pepper together in a large bowl and stir in the boiling stock and water until the mixture is very moist and smooth.

Wet the tamale papers individually, so that they do not stick together. Lay them out on a large surface—a kitchen table is best—so that the lines of the paper run horizontally in front of you. Place a tablespoon of the mush mixture about an inch from the edge of the tamale paper nearest you and spread it out gently with your finger to a length of about 4 inches. Top it with a lump of the meat mixture about the size of your little finger (about 1 ounce). Fold the paper over the meat and mush, tuck it in tight, and roll the tamale, folding the end of the paper in to seal the stuffing completely. Place the tamale in a large (5-gallon) stockpot. Continue rolling and stacking the tamales until the pot is three-quarters full. Add to the pot:

6 quarts beef stock (from above)   *3 tablespoons chili powder*
3 tablespoons paprika   *2 teaspoons salt*

Add enough beef stock to cover the tamales; if necessary, add water to cover. Cover the pot, place over high heat, and bring to a boil. Reduce the heat to medium-low and let the tamales simmer for about 2 hours. Check occasionally to be sure that the tamales are still covered with liquid; add more water as needed.

After 2 hours, test one of the tamales on top for doneness. Try another—you can never tell by just one. Or rather, you can't stop with one. Drain and serve.

You may freeze the tamales when they have cooled—pack in plastic freezer bags and spoon a little stock into each bag. They will freeze well for up to 6 months.

Makes 30 dozen.

Vegetables and Side Dishes

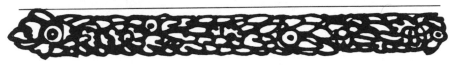

In southern Louisiana, we fix our vegetables as uniquely as we fix our gumbos and jambalayas. The abundance of fresh produce growing in our backyards for the past two hundred years made it easier for each generation to experiment and create dishes. Now, thanks to refrigeration and modern growing techniques, anyone can get a variety of fresh vegetables all year long, so it's our pleasure to show you how to prepare Cajun home-style vegetables, now that you have the ingredients. In particular, try Smothered Snap Beans, Maque Choux (Indian name for a smothered corn dish), Sweet Potato Praline Casserole (fix at least once a month), and Cajun Stuffed Tomatoes. You'll discover that the long cooking times typical of Cajun cooking apply here, too. True, the vegetables will be tender before that, but the different flavor Cajuns aim for is brought out only with prolonged cooking. Give it a try—you'll see. Come to this chapter with the same enthusiasm you approach the seafood and gumbo chapters and you'll walk away with a whole new outlook on corn, beans, and tomatoes.

❧ SMOTHERED SNAP BEANS ❧ WITH BACON AND NEW POTATOES

You may find yourself serving this side dish as a main dish on occasion, it's such a wonderful mixture of tastes and textures. But don't neglect to serve it with pork roast, smothered steak, game, or poultry. It doesn't look too pretty, but it sure does taste good.

1 pound fresh snap or green beans	*4 new potatoes*
	Salt to taste
5 slices bacon, halved	*2 teaspoons ground black pepper*
2 medium onions, chopped fine	*4 cups water*

Snap off the ends of the beans and wash them well. Place a Dutch oven or other large heavy pot over medium heat, add the bacon, and cook it slowly, until it is slightly browned but still soft. Add the beans, onions, potatoes, salt, pepper, and water. Stir well and bring to a simmer. Reduce heat, cover, and cook slowly, stirring occasionally, until the beans are very tender, about 1 hour. Add additional water if necessary to keep the mixture from drying out. Uncover the pot and mash the potatoes well. Raise the heat to medium-high and stir constantly until all the water has evaporated.

Serves 6–8.

❧ WHITE BEANS AND RICE ☙

This classic Cajun dish can stand on its own as a main course. It also makes an excellent side dish to accompany meat or poultry—I especially like to serve it with Smothered Round Steak or pork chops.

1 pound dried white or navy beans	*2 teaspoons salt*
1 pound tasso, fresh smoked sausage, or cured ham	*1 teaspoon ground black pepper*
	¹/₂ teaspoon ground red pepper
2 medium onions, chopped fine	*¹/₂ teaspoon ground white pepper*
1 large bell pepper, chopped fine	*2 cups chopped green onions*
	1 cup chopped parsley

It is best to soak the beans overnight in water to cover, but it is not essential—unsoaked beans simply take longer to cook.

If you are using tasso or ham, cut it in ¹/₂-inch dice; if you are using sausage, slice it ¹/₂ inch thick. Place the beans in a Dutch oven or other large heavy pot and add water to cover by about 2 inches. Bring to a boil and add the onions, bell pepper, tasso, ham, or sausage, salt, and peppers. Reduce the heat to medium and let simmer, stirring occasionally, until the beans are tender. Soaked beans will take 1–1¹/₂ hours, unsoaked beans up to 3 hours. If the mixture begins to dry out, add more water.

When the beans are tender, remove 2–3 cups of them, mash with a fork, and return to the pot. This makes a thick gravy base for the beans. If there still seems to be a lot of liquid in the pot, mash another couple of batches of beans the same way. Stir in the green onions and parsley and serve over rice.

Serves 6–8 as a main course, 10–12 as a side dish.

RED BEANS (OR CROWDER BEANS, FIELD PEAS, OR
BLACKEYED PEAS) AND RICE

Substitute any of these beans, fresh or dried, for the white or navy
beans and proceed as above. Fresh beans or peas will take less time,
naturally.

WHITE BEAN AND TASSO SOUP

Try this in cold weather, when you're in the mood for a hearty
main-dish soup. Proceed as above, but add more water—cover the
beans by 4 inches instead of 2. Don't worry about getting the
consistency just right until the end, though. Then mash more of
the beans, and add additional water until you reach the desired
consistency. This works equally well with red beans.

❧ MAQUE CHOUX ☙

This is one of those recipes that takes an ordinary ingredient and
transforms its taste and texture entirely. Try it just once, and I
guarantee you'll never fix corn any other way (except maybe boiling
it every now and then).

2 dozen ears fresh sweet corn
1 cup (¹/₂ pound) butter
2 medium onions, chopped fine
2 large bell peppers, chopped fine

6 large ripe tomatoes, peeled,
   seeded, and roughly chopped
2 teaspoons salt
2 teaspoons ground black pepper

Shuck the corn. Working with one cob at a time, hold over a bowl
and cut away the kernels in layers (you don't want to end up with
whole kernels), then scrape the knife down the cob to "milk" it.
    Heat the butter in a Dutch oven or other large heavy pot over

medium-high heat. Add the onions, bell peppers, and tomatoes and sauté until onions are transparent, about 15 minutes. Stir in the salt and pepper, then add the corn and the milk from the cobs and stir well. Reduce heat to medium and cook until the corn is tender, 20–30 minutes. If the mixture begins to dry out before the corn is tender, add a little milk and a little more butter.

Serves 6–8.

❧ SMOTHERED OKRA ☙

A basic Cajun side dish that makes a terrific accompaniment to almost any entrée. You may recognize the technique from the okra-based gumbo recipes earlier in this book—it follows the same basic method. It also freezes very well.

2 pounds fresh okra
2 medium onions,
  chopped fine
2 medium bell peppers,
  chopped fine

6 very ripe tomatoes, peeled,
  seeded, and roughly chopped
Salt and pepper to taste
3 cups water
1 teaspoon white vinegar

Wash the okra well and drain it. Cut off the stem ends and discard, then slice the okra thin. Place it in a Dutch oven or other large heavy pot, add the onions, bell peppers, tomatoes, salt and pepper, water, and vinegar and stir well. Cover and bring to a simmer over medium heat. Reduce heat and let simmer slowly until the okra is tender, 45 minutes to 1 hour, adding a little water if the okra seems to be drying out. If there seems to be too much liquid left in the pot, uncover, raise heat, and let some of it evaporate.

Serves 6–8.

❧ PETITS POIS ☙

Petits Pois is the traditional accompaniment to a lot of Cajun dishes, particularly Maw Maw's Chicken Stew. We always use canned peas, but try it with fresh ones if they're available—just increase the cooking time at the end.

1 can (16½ ounce) petits pois
2 tablespoons butter
1 small onion, minced

2 medium fresh mushrooms, chopped
Salt
Ground black pepper

Drain the peas. Melt the butter in a medium saucepan over medium-high heat, add the onion and mushrooms, and sauté until soft, 10–15 minutes. Just before serving, add the peas and salt and pepper to taste and let cook 3–4 minutes, just long enough to heat through. Don't stir too much—the peas are delicate.

Serves 4–6.

ᲠᲔ FRIED SQUASH ᲒᲛ

Fried vegetables are becoming more and more popular, not only as a side dish but as an hors d'oeuvre to serve with cocktails. Here's a basic recipe to get you going. It works equally well with okra (fry them whole), eggplant, zucchini, mushrooms, and so on.

4 small yellow squash	*1 tablespoon salt*
1 cup corn flour	*1 teaspoon ground red pepper*
1/2 cup cornmeal	*1 teaspoon ground black pepper*
1 pint milk	*1/2 teaspoon ground white pepper*
3 eggs	*Vegetable oil for deep-frying*

Clean the squash well and slice ¾ inch thick. Mix together the corn flour and cornmeal. In a separate bowl, beat together the milk and eggs. Combine the salt and peppers in a small bowl and divide them between the corn flour-cornmeal mixture and the egg-milk mixture. Mix well.

Pour the oil into a Dutch oven, fryer, or other large heavy pot to a depth of at least 3 inches. Heat to 350°F. Dip the squash slices into the batter first, then into the corn flour-cornmeal mixture, turning to coat well. Drop into the hot oil, one by one. Fry until golden brown, 3–4 minutes. Drain on paper toweling and serve immediately.

Serves 6–8.

☜ BROCCOLI AND CAULIFLOWER AU GRATIN ☞

The cheese sauce in this recipe is based on a cream reduction rather than a flour base. Once you discover how much lighter and smoother a sauce this makes, you'll be trying it on all kinds of other vegetables—and potatoes, too.

2 bunches fresh broccoli	*2 teaspoons chopped fresh basil, or*
1 head fresh cauliflower	*¹/₂ teaspoon dried*
1 pint heavy cream	*2 teaspoons fresh thyme, or*
³/₄ teaspoon salt	*¹/₂ teaspoon dried*
¹/₄ teaspoon ground red pepper	*1 tablespoon chopped fresh*
¹/₄ teaspoon ground black pepper	*jalapeño pepper (optional)*
¹/₄ teaspoon ground white	*2 cups grated cheese (American,*
pepper	*Jack, Cheddar, or Swiss)*

Bring a large kettle of water to a boil. Trim the broccoli and add it and the cauliflower to the water and cook until not quite tender. Drain well and rinse with cold water to arrest the cooking. Cut into smaller pieces and place in a casserole dish large enough to hold them.

Pour the cream into a large skillet and place over medium-high heat. Once it begins to rise, stir until it comes to a boil. Then stir in the salt, peppers, herbs, and jalapeño, if desired. Let the sauce reduce over medium heat, stirring often, until it is thick but not too thick—it should drip from a spoon without clinging. Remove from heat and stir in the grated cheese until it is thoroughly melted. Pour the cheese sauce over the broccoli and cauliflower. (You may make the casserole in advance to this point and place it in the refrigerator for up to 2 days. Let it stand at room temperature for 2 hours before baking.)

Preheat the oven to 325°F. Place the casserole in the oven and bake until hot through and beginning to brown, about 20 minutes.

Serves 6–8.

❧ CAJUN BAKED TOMATO CASSEROLE ❧

Take full advantage of fresh tomatoes when they're at their late-summer peak with this recipe, which can be prepared in advance and even frozen for cooler seasons. Try using the tomato dressing to stuff individual whole tomatoes—you'll get double the tomato flavor and a gorgeous presentation, too.

8–10 *large very ripe tomatoes*	2 *garlic cloves, minced*
¼ *teaspoon sugar*	*Salt*
½ *pound ground beef*	*Ground black pepper*
2 *medium bell peppers,*	2 *cups bread crumbs*
chopped	*Grated Parmesan cheese*
2 *medium onions, chopped*	*(optional)*
1 *celery rib, chopped*	

Peel and seed the tomatoes and roughly chop them. Mix in the sugar. Place a large heavy skillet over medium-high heat, add the ground beef, and brown well. Pour off the excess fat, then add the bell peppers, onions, celery, and garlic and sauté over medium heat until the vegetables are tender, 15–20 minutes. Stir in the tomatoes and simmer over low heat for about 1 hour more. Season with salt and pepper to taste, then stir in all but ¼ cup of the bread crumbs. The dressing should be fairly stiff, so add additional bread crumbs if necessary.

Preheat the oven to 350°F. Butter a medium casserole or oven-proof dish. Pour in the tomato mixture and sprinkle with the remaining bread crumbs and Parmesan cheese, if desired. (You can prepare the casserole in advance and store in the refrigerator or freezer until ready to bake. Simply increase the baking time to allow extra time to heat it through.) Place in the oven and bake until hot through and beginning to brown, about 30 minutes. Serve as a side dish, to accompany just about anything.

Serves 8–10.

STUFFED TOMATOES

Prepare as above, but use the tomato dressing to fill the centers of 8–10 large ripe unpeeled tomatoes (cut off the tops and hollow out the insides). Place the stuffed tomatoes in a single layer in a baking dish or casserole and bake at 350°F until hot through and beginning to brown—these will take only 15–20 minutes if baked immediately, a bit longer if refrigerated first.

❧ SWEET POTATO CASSEROLE ☙ WITH PRALINE TOPPING

An easy-to-make casserole featuring two favorite Louisiana products that are widely available across the country—sweet potatoes (or yams) and pecans. What a combination! You'll enjoy this year-round, but particularly at holiday time, alongside your smoked or baked turkey.

5 large sweet potatoes or yams
1/2 cup (1/4 pound) butter, softened
1/2 cup sugar
2 eggs, beaten
1 teaspoon vanilla

1/3 cup milk
1/2 cup heavy cream
1 cup light brown sugar
1/3 cup melted butter
1 cup chopped pecans

Preheat the oven to 350°F. Scrub the sweet potatoes or yams well and place them in the oven. Bake until tender, about 40 minutes, and remove. When they are cool enough to handle, halve them and scoop out the insides into a large mixing bowl. Mash well. You should have about 3 cups. (You can also peel and cube the sweet potatoes or yams and cook them in a little water until tender in a covered saucepan. Or you can use leftover sweet potatoes or yams.)

Mix the softened butter into the mashed yams or sweet potatoes along with the sugar, eggs, vanilla, and milk. Pour the mixture into a baking pan or casserole dish.

Bring the cream to a simmer in a small saucepan. Add the brown sugar and stir until it dissolves. Cook the mixture over medium heat until it reaches the soft-ball stage on a candy thermometer. Remove from the heat and beat in the butter and the chopped pecans. Pour this mixture over the yams. Bake until very hot and beginning to brown.

Serves 6–8.

❦ SMOTHERED CAJUN HASH BROWNS ❦

I realize that you're convinced by now that we Cajuns will smother everything from an old belt to an old shoe. But there's nothing like this dish to prove how nicely smothering plays up contrasting flavors. And don't forget to lay this right next to fresh smothered sausage.

3 large white potatoes (we use Idaho)
2 cups vegetable oil
2 medium yellow onions, chopped fine
2 medium bell peppers, chopped fine
1 tablespoon salt
2 teaspoons ground red pepper
2 teaspoons ground black pepper
1 teaspoon ground white pepper
5–6 shots Tabasco sauce
2 cups water
2 cups chopped green onions
1 cup chopped parsley

Peel the potatoes and cut them in ½-inch cubes. Place the oil in a Dutch oven or other large heavy pot over high heat. When it begins to smoke, add the potatoes, being careful not to splatter your-self. Do not stir. Once the potatoes have browned on that side, flip them over and brown on the other. Remove from heat and drain off the oil. Add the onions, bell peppers, salt, peppers, Tabasco, and water. Mix well and bring to a simmer over medium-high heat. Reduce heat to low, cover, and let simmer, stirring occasionally, until potatoes are very tender, about 30 minutes. If there it still liquid in the pot, uncover and raise the heat to evaporate the excess, stirring constantly, but being careful not to break up the potatoes too much. Stir in the green onions and parsley, cover again, and remove from heat. Let stand for about 5 minutes. Serve with eggs or meat, any time of day.

Serves 6.

❧ STUFFED BAKED POTATOES ❧

Potatoes prepared this way are two steps beyond plain old baked potatoes—not only are they stuffed, but the stuffing rises up, giving you little soufflés that make a terrific presentation alongside almost any main dish, especially seafood. If you're too short on time or energy to stuff individual shells, bake the stuffing mixture in a casserole—it'll taste every bit as good.

4 large baking potatoes (we use Idaho)
1/2 cup (1/4 pound) butter, melted
1 cup heavy cream
2 tablespoons sour cream
1 cup finely chopped tasso or crumbled bacon, fried
1 cup chopped green onions
6–8 shots Tabasco

1/2 cup chopped parsley
1 tablespoon salt
1 teaspoon ground red pepper
1 teaspoon ground black pepper
1 teaspoon ground white pepper
1 cup grated cheese (American, Jack, Cheddar)

Preheat the oven to 400°F. Scrub the potatoes and butter the outside, if you like. Bake them until done, 40 minutes to 1 hour. Remove and let cool. When they are cool enough to handle, halve them lengthwise and scoop the insides into a mixing bowl, leaving the shells intact. Mix in the butter, cream, sour cream, tasso or bacon, green onions, Tabasco, parsley, salt, and peppers. Mix well, but don't mash. Place the reserved shells on a cookie sheet and stuff with the potato mixture. Top evenly with the cheese. You may prepare the potatoes in advance to this point, but don't bake until the last minute—the potatoes will rise up like miniature soufflés, but they'll fall if they're not served immediately.

Have the oven at 400°F. Bake the potatoes until they are brown and puffy, 20–25 minutes (longer if they have been refrigerated first). Serve immediately.

Serves 6–8.

❧ POTATO SALAD ❧

In Cajun country, we don't just serve potato salad alongside fried chicken—it's also a traditional accompaniment to a bowl of gumbo. No matter how you serve it, though, be sure to use homemade mayonnaise; the flavor is incomparable, and it's a great way to discover just how easy mayonnaise really is.

5 medium red potatoes
4 eggs
2 tablespoons yellow mustard
1¹/₂ cups homemade mayonnaise
  (see following recipe)
1 medium bell pepper,
  chopped fine
1 large dill pickle, chopped
2 celery ribs, chopped fine

1 cup chopped green onions
¹/₂ cup chopped parsley
¹/₂ cup sweet pickle relish
  (optional)
1 tablespoon salt
1 teaspoon ground red pepper
2 teaspoons ground black pepper
1 teaspoon ground white pepper
4 shots Tabasco sauce

Bring a large saucepan of water to a boil. Add the potatoes and the eggs, return to a simmer, and reduce the heat so that the water is barely bubbling. Remove the eggs after 15 minutes and place them immediately in cold water to arrest the cooking. Continue to cook the potatoes until they are *just* tender. Drain them and let them cool. When they are cool enough to handle, peel them and cut in 1-inch cubes. Peel the eggs and separate the whites from the yolks. Chop the whites coarse and add them to the potatoes. Mash the yolks with the mustard and 2 tablespoons of the mayonnaise, then add to the potatoes. Add the rest of the ingredients and mix well.

Serves 8–10.

❧ MAYONNAISE ☙

2 egg yolks
1 teaspoon salt
1 garlic glove, minced
½ cup finely chopped green onions

4 shots Tabasco sauce
Juice of ½ lemon
2 cups high-grade
   vegetable oil

Place all the ingredients except the oil in a blender (with the center of the lid removed) or a food processor fitted with a plastic blade and blend or process for 2 minutes. Pour the oil in a very thin stream through the top or down the feed tube until it has all been incorporated. Blend or process for 30 seconds more.

Makes about 2½ cups.

Sweets

There's a good reason why this chapter is close to my heart. Not only am I as much of a dessert lover as everyone else, but Louisiana is sugarcane country, and Patouts own and run the oldest sugar plantation in the country still in operation. What's particularly nice about having sugarcane nearby is the wonderful raw sugar that's available. Add to that our sweet native pecans, Ruston peaches, and Hammond strawberries, and the customary care Cajuns lavish on food, and you'll understand why our desserts shine on their own, rather than taking a backseat to the rest of our cooking.

We particularly like to feature our sweets in a big way—by themselves for an afternoon treat with coffee, or as part of a lavish holiday spread. Our cookies and pies are a mainstay of the Fourth of July and Labor Day, Thanksgiving and Christmas—times of celebration when we like to pull out the stops and have the leisure to spend as long fixing sweetmeats as in preparing the main courses. Packed in colorful tins, many of the cookies and candies in this chapter make excellent holiday gifts for family and friends. In warm weather, an old-fashioned ice cream picnic is a nice way to bring family together. And among our recipes—many of them family favorites handed down through the generations—are cakes, pies, and puddings that make rich, homey endings to a light supper, or sophisticated finales for your most elegant company dinners. You don't need a special occasion to turn on the oven and get out the cake pans or cookie sheets, though—a plain old hankering for something sweet and satisfying is a good enough excuse.

❦ OLD DOMINION POUND CAKE ❦

This is a special-occasion cake that we like to serve with whipped cream. It mellows with age, so make it at least one day ahead of serving. It keeps very well in the refrigerator for several days and freezes beautifully.

8 large eggs, at room temperature
2¼ cups sifted all-purpose flour
¼ teaspoon baking soda
2¼ cups sugar
1½ cups (¾ pound) butter, at room temperature

2 tablespoons lemon juice
2¼ teaspoons vanilla
⅛ teaspoon salt
1½ teaspoons cream of tartar
1 cup very finely chopped walnuts
Confectioners' sugar

Preheat the oven to 350°F. Butter and flour a Bundt or tube pan.

Separate the eggs. Sift the flour with the baking soda and 1¼ cups of the sugar. Place the butter in the bowl of an electric mixer and cream it well. Beat in the flour-sugar mixture by thirds, then beat in the lemon juice and vanilla. Beat in the egg yolks one by one, being sure each is absorbed before you add the next.

In a separate mixing bowl, beat the egg whites until frothy. Add the salt and the cream of tartar and continue beating until soft peaks form. Gradually beat in the remaining 1 cup sugar, and continue beating until the mixture is glossy and holds stiff peaks.

Fold the nuts into the flour mixture, then gently fold in the beaten egg whites. Turn the batter into the prepared pan and gently cut through the batter once or twice with a rubber spatula to break up any large air bubbles.

Bake the cake for 1½ hours, or until a knife or toothpick inserted near the center comes out clean. Do not open the oven during the first hour of baking. Turn off the heat and let the cake sit in the hot oven for 15 minutes. Then remove and let cool in the pan for 15 minutes more. Remove the cake from the pan and sprinkle lightly with confectioners' sugar. Let cool thoroughly, then wrap tight in foil.

Serve in thin slices, with whipped cream, if desired.

✎ FUDGE CAKE ✎

This cake is for chocolate lovers, and is delicious topped with vanilla ice cream. The recipe is one of the first that was used in Daddy's restaurant at the Hotel Frederic, and it was served every day until the restaurant closed.

½ cup (¼ pound) butter	*2 eggs*
4 ounces unsweetened baking	*½ cup all-purpose flour*
chocolate	*1 teaspoon vanilla*
1 cup sugar	*2 cups coarsely chopped pecans*

Preheat the oven to 350°F. Butter a 13 × 7-inch baking pan.

Melt the butter and chocolate over very low heat. Stir to combine and let cool.

Beat together the sugar and eggs until very light. Mix in the chocolate-butter mixture. Then stir in the flour, vanilla, and pecans. Pour into the prepared baking pan and place in the oven.

Bake for about 35 minutes, or until a knife or toothpick inserted near the center comes out clean. Remove from oven and let cool in pan.

Icing

1¹/₂ cups confectioners' sugar   *¹/₄ cup milk*
3 tablespoons cocoa   *2 tablespoons butter*

Sift together the confectioners' sugar and the cocoa into a mixing bowl. Heat the milk and butter together in a small saucepan until the butter is melted, then stir it into the sugar-cocoa mixture until the icing reaches the consistency of heavy cream. Spread the icing on the cooled cake. Serve cut in squares.

At least 2 dozen servings.

☜ PINEAPPLE UPSIDE-DOWN CAKE ☞

Another favorite dessert from the Hotel Frederic restaurant.

¹/₂ cup (¹/₄ pound) butter, at room   *²/₃ cup milk*
   temperature   *1 teaspoon vanilla*
1 cup sugar   *1 cup dark brown sugar*
3 eggs, well beaten   *8 slices sweetened canned*
2 cups sifted cake flour   *pineapple*
3 teaspoons baking powder   *8 maraschino cherries*
¹/₂ teaspoon salt

Preheat the oven to 350°F. Butter a 10-inch cast-iron skillet or other heavy, round ovenproof pan.

Place the butter and sugar in the bowl of an electric mixer and cream them well. Beat in the eggs. Sift together the flour, baking powder, and salt and add to the batter alternately with the milk, in two stages. Gently fold in the vanilla.

Sprinkle the brown sugar evenly over the bottom of the prepared skillet or pan. Arrange the slices of pineapple in a single layer over the sugar and place a cherry in the center of each. Pour the batter over. Place the cake in the oven and bake for 40–45 minutes, or until a knife or toothpick inserted near the center comes out clean. Remove the cake and let it cool completely. Then invert it onto a cake plate and serve.

Serves 8.

❧ GÂTEAU AU SIROP (SYRUP CAKE) ❧

This is a real Cajun cake, excellent served hot with whipped cream. If you want to go whole hog, serve it after a brunch of Grillades and grits.

2½ cups all-purpose flour
½ cup chopped pecans
½ cup raisins
1½ teaspoons double-acting baking powder
½ teaspoon baking soda
½ teaspoon salt
1 teaspoon ground ginger
1 teaspoon cinnamon

¼ teaspoon ground nutmeg
¼ teaspoon ground cloves
1 cup pure cane syrup, or substitute ⅔ cup dark corn syrup
1 cup boiling water
½ cup (¼ pound) butter, softened
½ cup sugar
2 eggs

Preheat the oven to 350°F. Butter and flour a 9-inch square baking pan.

Sprinkle a little of the flour over the pecans and raisins and set aside. Sift the rest of the flour with the baking powder, baking soda, salt, ginger, cinnamon, nutmeg, and cloves. In a separate bowl, combine the cane or corn syrup and water.

In a large mixing bowl, cream the butter and sugar until fluffy. Beat in the eggs, one at a time. Beat in the sifted dry ingredients by thirds, alternating with the syrup mixture in two parts. Beat well after each addition. Gently fold in the pecans and raisins. Pour the batter into the prepared pan and place in the oven. Bake for 55 minutes, or until a knife or toothpick inserted near the center comes out clean. Remove. You can let this cake cool before serving, but it is also delicious hot. Either way, it's great cut in squares and served with whipped cream.

❦ BREAD PUDDING ❧

Even when you're using up leftovers, you can cook with elegance. For a really special presentation, bake this pudding in individual soufflé cups or ramekins. It is delicious both warm and cold.

1 loaf stale French bread
2 cups milk
3 eggs, beaten
1 teaspoon vanilla
1 tablespoon cinnamon
1/2 cup raw white or brown sugar

1 cup raisins
1 cup chopped canned pineapple
1/2 cup (1/4 pound) butter, melted
1/4 teaspoon salt
1/2 cup chopped walnuts or pecans
  (optional)

Preheat the oven to 350°F.

Tear the bread into small pieces and place in a bowl. Cover with the milk and let soak 15–20 minutes. Then mash the bread to get rid of any remaining chunks. Add the eggs, vanilla, cinnamon, sugar, raisins, pineapple, butter, salt, and nuts, if desired, and mix well. Pour into a buttered 8- or 9-inch square or round baking pan and bake for about 45 minutes, until set in the middle and browned on top. Cut in wedges or squares and serve with sweetened whipped cream, flavored, if desired, with Grand Marnier or brandy.

❦ BLACKBERRY PIE ❧

On Saturday mornings around the end of April and beginning of May, we'd get so antsy that Mama would hand us each a bucket and tell us not to come back until they were filled with blackberries. In return, she'd promise to make us a blackberry pie that evening. If you live where fresh blueberries are available, send your children out for some of them to try in this recipe.

4 cups fresh blackberries
2 cups sugar
3 tablespoons cornstarch
1/4 teaspoon salt

1 recipe Pie Dough
  (see following recipe)
3 tablespoons butter

Preheat the oven to 425°F.

Wash and pick over the blackberries. Sprinkle with the sugar, cornstarch, and salt and mix well. Line an 8- or 9-inch pie pan with the pastry. Fill two-thirds full with blackberries and dot with the butter. Roll out the rest of the pastry as directed to form a top crust, place it over the berries, and crimp around the edges to seal well. Cut several 2-inch gashes in the top to allow the steam to escape. Bake in the middle of the oven for 1 hour. If the crust begins to brown too fast around the edges, cover with aluminum foil and continue baking.

Makes one 8- or 9-inch pie.

❧ PIE DOUGH ❧

2 cups all-purpose
   flour
³/₄ teaspoon salt

²/₃ cup solid vegetable shortening,
   such as Crisco
About ¹/₂ cup ice water

Sift the flour and salt together into a mixing bowl. Cut in the shortening with a pastry cutter, a fork, or your fingers until the mixture is like cornmeal. Stir in just enough water that the mixture holds together. Gather the dough into a ball and chill it for at least 30 minutes.

Divide the dough in two portions. Roll out one portion on a lightly floured surface and use it to line an 8- or 9-inch pie pan, trimming away the excess. Fill as directed. If you are making a single-crust pie, freeze the remaining dough (or make two pies!). Or use the extra dough to make a top crust or lattice. Bake as directed.

Makes enough pastry for 2 single-crust or 1 double-crust 8- or 9-inch pies.

❧ PECAN PIE ❧

A very popular dessert in our part of the country, thanks to the abundance of pecans. We like it best served warm.

1 recipe Pie Dough (see preceding recipe)
3 eggs
³/₄ cup sugar
1 cup dark corn syrup
¹/₈ teaspoon salt

2 tablespoons butter or margarine, melted
1 teaspoon vanilla
1 cup pecan pieces
10–12 pecan halves

Preheat the oven to 350°F. Line an 8- or 9-inch pie pan with the pie dough.

Place the eggs in a mixing bowl and beat them lightly. Beat in the sugar, corn syrup, salt, butter, and vanilla. Fold in the pecan pieces. Pour into the pie shell and bake until partly set, about 15 minutes. Remove from the oven and garnish with the pecan halves. Return the pie to the oven and bake until a knife or toothpick inserted near the center comes out clean, 20–25 minutes more. Remove and let cool. Serve warm or cool, with vanilla ice cream or whipped cream.

Makes one 8- or 9-inch pie.

❧ RUSSIAN ROCKS ❧

These cookies, along with Icebox Cookies and Cocoons, are our traditional holiday cookies. They can all be made a couple of weeks ahead and stored in tins—well hidden!

1½ teaspoons baking soda
3 tablespoons boiling water
3 cups all-purpose flour
4 cups raisins, dark or golden
3 cups coarsely chopped pecans
½ teaspoon salt

1 teaspoon cinnamon
1 teaspoon ground allspice
½ cup (¼ pound) butter, at room temperature
1½ cups sugar
3 eggs, separated

Preheat the oven to 350°F. Grease a cookie sheet or two.

Dissolve the baking soda in the boiling water and let cool. Sprinkle a little of the flour over the raisins and pecans and set aside. Sift the rest of the flour with the salt, cinnamon, and allspice.

Cream the butter and sugar well. Beat in the egg yolks, one by one. Then stir in the sifted dry ingredients. In a separate bowl, beat the egg whites until they form stiff peaks. Fold them into the batter, then fold in the dissolved baking soda and, last of all, the raisins and pecans.

Drop the batter by half-teaspoonfuls onto the cookie sheet about an inch apart. Bake 10–12 minutes, or until lightly browned. Remove to a rack to cool. Store in tightly covered tins, or in plastic containers lined with waxed paper.

Makes 6–7 dozen.

❧ ICEBOX COOKIES ❧

This is my all-time favorite cookie. After all, the only reason we have Thanksgiving is so we can serve smoked turkey and icebox cookies!

1 pound light brown sugar
2 cups (1 pound) butter, at room
   temperature
1 egg, well beaten
1 teaspoon vanilla

6 cups sifted all-purpose
   flour
1 teaspoon baking powder
1 teaspoon salt
1 cup ground pecans

Cream together the sugar and butter. Beat in the egg and vanilla. Sift the flour with the baking powder and salt and combine with the ground pecans. Blend this mixture into the creamed butter mixture in two parts—you will be able to stir in the first part, but the second you will probably have to work in by hand. The dough will be very stiff. Divide it into 6 equal portions. Roll each into a cylinder 1–1½ inches in diameter, wrap in waxed paper, and chill overnight.

Preheat the oven to 350°F. Butter a couple of cookie sheets.

Slice each cylinder of dough into rounds, as thin as possible. Place the rounds close together on the cookie sheets and bake them for about 8 minutes, until they are very lightly browned. Cool on racks. Stored in tightly covered tins, these cookies would probably keep for weeks if they weren't eaten first.

Makes at least 10 dozen tiny wafers.

❧ COCOONS ❧

This is one of Mo Mo's recipes for a pecan shortbread.

1 cup (½ pound) butter, at room
temperature
3 level tablespoons confectioners'
sugar
3 scant cups all-purpose flour

1 teaspoon vanilla
2 cups ground (or very
finely chopped)
pecans
Confectioners' sugar

Preheat the oven to 350°F and butter a cookie sheet or two.

Cream the butter with the sugar and blend in the flour. Mix in the vanilla and pecans.

Roll the dough into ¾-inch balls and place them on the cookie sheets about an inch apart. Place in the oven and bake for about 15 minutes—they should be dry but not at all brown. Roll the cookies in powdered sugar, then transfer to racks and let cool. Store tightly covered.

Makes about 5 dozen.

❧ LES OREILLES DE COCHON ❧
(PIG'S EARS)

Another true Acadian sweet, good for a pick-me-up or coffee break as well as after a meal.

2 cups all-purpose flour
¹/₂ tablespoon salt
¹/₂ teaspoon baking powder
1 teaspoon solid vegetable
  shortening, such as Crisco

²/₃ cup milk
Vegetable oil for deep-frying
2 cups pure cane syrup, or
  substitute dark corn syrup
1 cup coarsely chopped pecans

Sift together the flour, salt, and baking powder into a large bowl. Cut in the shortening. Add the milk and mix well until the dough holds together.

Lightly flour a work surface. Pinch off a piece of dough about the size of a walnut and roll it out into a very thin square about 4 × 4 inches, or into a circle about 6 inches in diameter. Repeat with the rest of the dough, stacking the squares or circles with pieces of waxed paper between each layer.

Pour the oil into a deep skillet, Dutch oven, or fryer to a depth of at least 1¹/₂ inches. Heat to 350°F. Armed with a two-pronged barbecue fork, drop in a square (or circle) of dough; immediately pierce the center with the fork and give it a twist to gather the dough toward the center in folds. Fry until lightly browned, about 30 seconds a side. (You won't be able to fry more than one or two at a time.) Drain on paper toweling.

Heat the cane or corn syrup in a small saucepan and stir in the pecans. Dribble about 2 tablespoons over the top of each pastry. Serve at room temperature. Store in a tightly sealed tin.

Makes about 2 dozen.

❧ PRALINE COOKIES ❧

These are very delicate, crispy cookies that look like lace and have a wonderful dark sugar flavor. Don't try doubling the recipe—it doesn't work well in larger amounts. If you want more—and you very well may—make another batch.

*1 cup brown sugar
(light, dark, or a
mixture)
1 tablespoon all-purpose flour*

*Dash of salt
1 egg white
1 teaspoon vanilla
2 cups pecan halves*

Preheat the oven to 325°F. Grease a cookie sheet or two very well.

Break up any lumps in the sugar and mix in the flour and salt. Beat the egg white until stiff but not dry and fold in. Fold in the vanilla and pecans. The dough should cling to the nuts. Drop the dough by small teaspoonfuls onto the cookie sheets, leaving about 2 inches between. Bake for about 20 minutes, or until lightly browned. Remove from the cookie sheets immediately and cool on racks. Should a cookie stick to the sheet, return it to the oven for a few seconds to loosen it.

Makes about 2 dozen.

❦ GRANDMOTHER'S SUGAR COOKIES ❧

Here's a treat for the little ones—a good basic cookie.

1 cup solid vegetable shortening, such as Crisco
2 cups sugar
2 eggs, beaten
1/2 teaspoon baking soda

3/4 cup thick sour milk or buttermilk
3 cups all-purpose flour
1 teaspoon salt
1 teaspoon nutmeg

Preheat the oven to 350°F. Grease a couple of cookie sheets.

Cream the shortening with 1½ cups of the sugar. Beat in the eggs. Dissolve the baking soda in the sour milk or buttermilk and mix in. Combine the flour and salt and stir in. Mix well.

Drop the dough by teaspoonfuls onto the cookie sheets, leaving about 2 inches between cookies. Combine the remaining ½ cup sugar and the nutmeg and sprinkle lightly over each. Bake for about 10 minutes, until delicately browned around the edges. Cool on racks. Store in tightly sealed containers.

Makes about 4 dozen.

❧ CALAS ❧

These tender, golden rice fritters are one of Louisiana's most famous sweets.

2½ cups cold cooked rice
¾ cup all-purpose flour
¼ cup sugar
2 teaspoons grated lemon rind
½ teaspoon salt

¼ teaspoon nutmeg
3 eggs
1 package active dry yeast
Vegetable oil for deep-frying
Confectioners' sugar

Place the rice in a large mixing bowl. Stir in the flour, sugar, lemon rind, salt, and nutmeg. Beat the eggs with the yeast and stir in. Beat well. Cover the bowl with a dish towel and let it stand in a warm place (80–85°F) for about 1 hour. The batter will become thick and foamy.

Pour the oil into a large heavy skillet to a depth of at least 1 inch. Heat to 375°F. Carefully drop the batter into the hot oil by rounded tablespoonfuls; fry only a few at a time. Fry until golden brown, turning once (about 2 minutes on each side). Drain on paper toweling and sprinkle with confectioners' sugar. Serve warm.

Makes about 2 dozen.

❧ LEMON ICE CREAM ❧

We have used this recipe forever. It makes a wonderful excuse for a family get-together as well as a refreshing dessert.

3¹/₄ cups sugar
2 quarts milk
2 pints heavy cream

1¹/₄ cups freshly squeezed
    lemon juice

Combine 1½ cups of the sugar with the milk and stir until dissolved. Chill. Whip the cream until it forms soft peaks. Place the sweetened milk and the whipped cream in an ice cream freezer and begin to freeze according to the manufacturer's instructions. When the cream mixture is thoroughly chilled and has begun to thicken, add the lemon juice and the rest of the sugar and finish freezing. You can also add 1 lemon—rind and all—seeded and chopped fine.

Makes about 1 gallon.

❧ OLD-FASHIONED CUSTARD ICE CREAM ❧

This ice cream is delicious plain, but for a dessert that is truly out of this world, try it with Old Dominion Pound Cake. This recipe also makes an incomparable base for fresh fruit ice creams.

8 eggs
2½ cups sugar
2 tablespoons all-purpose flour
½ teaspoon salt

2½ quarts milk
2 cans (12 ounce) evaporated
  milk, chilled
2 teaspoons vanilla

Beat together the eggs, sugar, flour, and salt. Scald 1½ quarts of the milk in a medium saucepan. Beat a little of the hot milk into the egg-sugar mixture, then whisk this mixture back into the rest of the milk and cook, stirring constantly, over medium-low heat until the custard has become very thick—it should drop from a spoon in globs. Let the custard cool completely, then chill it.

When you are ready to freeze the ice cream, blend the evaporated milk into the custard and add the vanilla. Pour into the cylinder of an ice cream freezer and add enough of the remaining milk to reach the fill line. Freeze according to the manufacturer's directions.

Makes 4–5 quarts.

FRESH PEACH OR STRAWBERRY ICE CREAM

Prepare as above, but reduce the sugar to 2 cups and add 1 quart crushed strawberries or peaches to the ice cream instead of the additional milk. If you are making peach ice cream, substitute 2 teaspoons almond extract for the vanilla.

❧ HEAVENLY HASH ❧

You don't need a special excuse to make this or any of the other candies that follow—a good supply of shelled pecans, a cold, rainy day when everybody's indoors and looking for something to pass the time, or just an aching sweet tooth are reasons enough.

*1 package (12 ounce) semisweet
    chocolate pieces*
1 can (14 ounce) condensed milk

2 cups pecan pieces
*1 package (10 ounce) miniature
    marshmallows*

Thoroughly butter a 9 × 13-inch pan.

Place the chocolate pieces in a large saucepan over very low heat (or in a double boiler) just long enough to melt. Add the condensed milk and mix well. Fold in the pecans and marshmallows and pour into the prepared dish. Spread evenly and let stand until firm, then cut in 2-inch squares.

Makes about 2 dozen.

❧ CHOCOLATE FUDGE ❧

4 cups sugar
2/3 cup cocoa
2 tablespoons light corn syrup
2/3 cup milk

2/3 cup evaporated milk
1/2 cup (1/4 pound) butter
1 teaspoon vanilla
3 cups coarsely chopped pecans

Thoroughly butter a 9-inch square pan.

In a large heavy saucepan, combine the sugar and cocoa. Stir in the corn syrup, milk, and evaporated milk. Bring to a boil over medium-high heat and continue cooking until it reaches the soft-ball stage (236°F on a candy thermometer). Remove from heat and let cool for 2–3 minutes, then beat in the butter and vanilla. Beat rapidly for several minutes, then stir in the pecans. Pour into the prepared pan and let cool until firm. Cut in small squares.

Makes at least 2 dozen pieces.

❦ PRALINES ❦

This recipe makes the creamiest pralines anywhere.

2 cups heavy cream
4 cups raw or brown
* sugar*

1 teaspoon vanilla
2 cups pecan halves
2 tablespoons butter

Butter a medium saucepan—this will make it easier to clean later. Pour in the cream and place over high heat. When it begins to boil, add the sugar and stir rapidly until it dissolves. Then stir in the vanilla and pecans and continue to cook over medium heat, stirring frequently, until the mixture reaches the soft-ball stage (236°F on a candy thermometer). Remove from heat and quickly beat in the butter—this helps arrest the cooking process. The candy should lose its glossy color and become very cloudy.

Lay out a long strip of waxed paper on a work surface. Moisten it with a damp towel. Drop good-size spoonfuls of the hot praline mixture onto the waxed paper, stirring the mixture occasionally as you go along to keep it well combined. Remove the pralines from the paper before they have cooled completely—later on it will be hard to remove them without breaking them. Store in tightly sealed containers, with layers of waxed paper in between.

Makes about 2 dozen.

❧ PEANUT BRITTLE ☙

2 cups shelled raw peanuts
1 cup sugar
½ cup light corn syrup

½ cup water
1 heaping teaspoon baking
  soda

In a medium saucepan, combine the peanuts, sugar, corn syrup, and water and bring to a boil over medium heat. Continue cooking over medium-low heat until the mixture begins to caramelize (at about 300°F on a candy thermometer). The cooking process should take about 30 minutes—you'll know that you're almost done when the nuts begin to pop and split in half. Quickly beat in the baking soda.

Pour the peanut mixture onto a greased marble slab or length of aluminum foil and let cool. When the brittle is completely cool, break it in pieces. Store in tightly sealed tins or containers.

❧ DIVINITY ☙

Daddy's sister Edele was the family's official divinity maker, and this is her recipe. This candy is traditional for Christmas and for bridal showers. Choose a dry day to make it.

4 cups sugar
1 cup light corn syrup
1 cup water

4 egg whites
2 cups pecan pieces

In a heavy saucepan, mix together the sugar, corn syrup, and water and bring to a boil over medium-high heat. Boil until it reaches the hard-crack stage (290°F on a candy thermometer). Beat the egg whites until stiff and pour the syrup over, beating constantly (this is easier with two people). Fold in the pecans. Drop by spoonfuls onto waxed paper and let stand until dry, 10–15 minutes. Peel the candies from the paper and store in airtight tins.

Makes at least 4 dozen.

❧ DATE ROLL ☙

Another holiday sweet that keeps very well.

2 cups sugar
1 cup milk
1 package (8 ounce) pitted dates,
    sliced

2 tablespoons butter
3 cups finely chopped
    pecans
1 teaspoon vanilla

In a heavy saucepan, mix together the sugar and milk. Bring to a boil over medium-high heat and cook until it reaches the soft-ball stage (236°F on a candy thermometer). Stir in the dates and return the mixture to the soft-ball stage. Remove from heat and beat in the butter. Then beat in the pecans and vanilla. Pour the candy onto a clean, damp dish towel. Roll it into a cylinder about 2 inches in diameter and let stand until cool and firm. Unwrap and slice about ¼ inch thick. Store in airtight tins.

Makes at least 2 dozen slices.

Pickles
and Preserves

There's a pickle or preserve for every time of day and every season. Nothing beats the taste of homemade Fig Preserves on hot biscuits with morning coffee, or tangy Chow Chow with thin slices of cured ham at suppertime. And putting up fruits and vegetables is a way of getting the best out of the year, of savoring the flavors of summer while you're eating hearty winter roasts and stews. You'll be happy to know that it's not difficult, either, if you follow a few simple rules.

Never use brass, copper, or tin utensils when soaking ingredients before pickling them. Glass is traditional, and plastic is also an excellent choice—we have used plastic ice chests with great success. Another modern convenience in home pickling is the dishwasher, which makes sterilizing jars by hand unnecessary. Just run them through on the wash cycle while your fruits or vegetables are cooking so that they'll still be hot when the pickles or preserves are ready to be packed. *Always* pack pickles and preserves while they are hot: Fill the jars up to the neck (leave about ¾ inch headroom) and seal immediately with new lids. The suction that occurs as the contents cool will create a nice tight seal.

❧ CHOW CHOW ❧

This relish makes a superb accompaniment to meats, particularly ham. We also use it as a sandwich spread. If you reduce the quantity of this recipe, you will also need to reduce the cooking times. But you probably won't want to go to the trouble of chopping up all those vegetables for less.

2 medium to large heads cabbage	*2 cups sugar*
12 large cucumbers	*8 ounces dry mustard*
2 large heads cauliflower	*2 cups olive oil*
About 2 dozen green tomatoes	*1 ounce turmeric, dissolved in*
5 large white onions	*1 quart white vinegar*
1½ cups salt	*Salt*
1 gallon white vinegar	*Pepper*
1½ quarts water	*Worcestershire sauce*
¾ cup flour	*Tabasco sauce*

Coarsely chop all the vegetables. (Do not peel or core the cucumbers or tomatoes.) You should end up with about a gallon each of cabbage, cucumbers, cauliflower, and tomatoes, and about a quart of onions.

Mix the vegetables with the salt in a large container, add water to cover, and let sit overnight or for at least 12 hours. Drain.

Bring 1½ quarts of the vinegar and the water to a boil in a large pot and add the vegetables. Return to the boil and cook over medium-high heat until tender, about 30 minutes. Drain and return to the pot.

Mix together the flour, sugar, and mustard. Stir in the olive oil and the turmeric-vinegar mixture. Bring the remaining 2½ quarts vinegar to a boil and stir in. Season to taste with salt, pepper, Worcestershire sauce, and Tabasco. Pour over the vegetables, bring to a boil, and cook over low heat until the liquid thickens (it should coat the spoon), about 25 minutes.

Pack in sterilized jars while hot and seal.

Makes about 24 pints.

❧ HOT PEPPER JELLY ❧

This jelly is delicious with all meats and very good with various cheeses as an appetizer on toast or crackers. You really have to have fresh, very hot peppers for this recipe, to balance the sugar. If you like your jelly really hot, leave the seeds in the hot peppers.

³/₄ cup seeded and roughly chopped bell pepper
¹/₄ cup seeded and roughly chopped hot peppers (tabasco, cayenne, or jalepeño)

6¹/₂ cups sugar
1¹/₂ cups cider vinegar
1 bottle (6 ounce) Certo (fruit pectin)
Few drops of red or green food coloring

Mince the peppers together very fine (or use a blender or food processor). You can leave them coarse if you like a chunkier jelly. Mix with the sugar and cider vinegar in a large saucepan and bring to a boil. Let boil down uncovered until thick like corn syrup. Remove from heat and let sit for 5 minutes. Add the Certo and stir thoroughly, then stir in a few drops food coloring. Pack while hot in sterilized jars (baby food jars make excellent containers for this) and seal.

Makes 3 to 4 pints.

⭑ FIG PRESERVES ⭑

We use our good local Celeste figs for this, but you can use what-ever variety is available fresh to you. Nobody makes fig preserve any better than Maw Maw, and here is her recipe.

7 pounds fresh figs   *¹/₂ cup water*
5 pounds sugar

Wash figs well and cut off stems. Place all ingredients in a large pot. Bring to a boil, lower heat, and simmer for 1–1¼ hours, or until the figs are transparent and the syrup coats the spoon thickly.
    Spoon while hot into sterilized half-pint or pint jars and seal.

Makes about 1 dozen pints.

⭑ SPICED PICKLED PEACHES ⭑

These are excellent with ham, poultry, or game.

10 pounds peaches   *2 cups cider vinegar*
Whole cloves   *3 cinnamon sticks*
4 pounds light brown sugar

Peel peaches and stick 3 cloves in each. Mix them with the brown sugar and let stand overnight in a cool place or refrigerate.
    Drain the liquid from the peaches into a saucepan and add the vinegar and cinnamon sticks. Bring to a boil. Drop the peaches into the boiling syrup a few at a time, letting the syrup return to the boil before adding more. Cook for 20 minutes, or until tender.
    Pack the peaches while hot into sterilized jars and seal.

Makes about 6 pints.

❧ BREAD AND BUTTER PICKLES ❧

25 small young cucumbers (about
   6 inches long)
12 small to medium white onions
2 cups salt
2 cups white vinegar

1½ cups sugar
1 tablespoon yellow mustard seed
1 tablespoon celery seed
2 teaspoons turmeric
2 teaspoons ground ginger

Wash the cucumbers but don't peel them. Slice the cucumbers and the onions about ⅛ inch thick. Mix them with the salt in a large container. Let stand 3 hours. Drain.

Bring the remaining ingredients to a boil in a large pot. (You can add salt if you like your pickles extra salty.) Add the onions and cucumbers, return to the boil, and boil hard for 3 minutes.

Pack while hot into sterilized jars and seal.

Makes about 1 dozen pints.

❧ MIXED MUSTARD PICKLES ❧

1 medium head cauliflower
3 medium green peppers
1 pound very small pearl
*   onions*
2 pounds green tomatoes
3 large cucumbers
2 cups very small cucumbers
*   (about 1½ inches long)*

1 cup salt
6 cups water
6 cups white vinegar
2 cups sugar
2 teaspoons celery seed
¼ cup flour
¾ teaspoon turmeric
¼ cup dry mustard

Wash the cauliflower and remove the green stalks. Break into florets. Halve and seed the peppers and slice into ¼-inch strips. Peel and halve the onions—if very small, leave whole. Cut the tomatoes into 8 wedges each. Wash the large cucumbers but do not peel; slice them ⅛ inch thick. Wash the small cucumbers and leave them whole.

Combine all the vegetables in a large heavy pot. Dissolve the salt in 4 cups of the water and pour over the vegetables. Let stand at room temperature 12 hours or overnight. Be sure the vegetables are covered with brine—add a little more water if necessary. Bring to a boil, lower heat, and simmer for 5 minutes. Drain.

In a separate saucepan combine the vinegar, sugar, and celery seed. Mix together the flour, turmeric, and mustard and slowly stir in the remaining 2 cups water. Stir this mixture into the vinegar mixture. Bring to a boil and cook over moderate heat, stirring constantly, until smooth and thick (it should coat the spoon). Add the vegetables and return to a boil, then lower heat and simmer for 15 minutes, stirring gently from time to time.

Pack while hot into sterilized jars and seal.

Makes about 8 pints.

Menus

I hope that as you get comfortable cooking Cajun, you'll begin to work the new tastes and techniques you're learning into your daily meals. But to help you get started, I've included some typical menus for eating Cajun throughout the year.

As in many parts of this country, Sunday dinner is the main meal of the week in Cajun country. Here are two menus my mother's mother, Maw Maw, likes to serve:

> Maw Maw's Chicken Stew
> Rice and Gravy
> Maque Choux
> Petits Pois
> Old-Fashioned Custard Ice Cream
>
> Boston Butt Pork Roast
> Rice and Gravy *or* Cajun Rice Dressing
> Smothered Snap Beans
> Cajun Baked Tomato Casserole
> Pineapple Upside-Down Cake

For a Monday supper we might use up Sunday dinner leftovers

in a jambalaya or have a simple, hearty meal of White Beans and Rice.

Shrimp Creole, Redfish Courtbouillon, Chicken and Sausage Gumbo, Cabbage Rolls, Rabbit Sauce Piquante, White Bean and Tasso Soup, and Chicken Pie all make excellent weekday lunches. For weekday suppers, we might dine on Eggplant Casserole or Cajun Seafood au Gratin, or one of the following menus:

Smothered Sausage
Cajun Hash Browns
Broccoli and Cauliflower au Gratin

Fried Fish with Homemade Tartar Sauce
Potato Salad with Homemade Mayonnaise
Hush Puppies

Smothered Chicken
Rice and Gravy *or* Cajun Rice Dressing
Smothered Okra
Fresh Blackeyed Peas

Friday night is the time for having friends to dinner, and to serve something special, like Crawfish Yvonne, Shrimp and Crab Étouffée, Baked Fish with Creole Sauce, Crawfish Bisque, or Boiled Crabs. For really festive dinners, we get more elaborate. Here are two menus we might serve:

Shrimp and Crab Stew
Stuffed Fish
Shrimp and Ham Jambalaya
Pecan Pie

Stuffed Mushrooms
Redfish Eugenie
Stuffed Baked Potatoes
Bread Pudding with Whipped Cream

Saturday noon is a good time for a quiet, lazy lunch, such as

Jambalaya Lafitte, Red Beans and Rice with homemade smoked sausage, or Smothered Round Steak with White Beans and Rice. But for Saturday night, we really like to pull out the stops! For example:

Shrimp Rémoulade
Oysters Alexander
Turtle Soup
Tournedos Patout
Blackberry Pie

Daube Glacé
Oysters Edele
Corn and Crab Bisque
Lady Fish
Pralines

And of course there's the classic Louisiana weekend brunch of Grillades and grits, which we'd accompany with an omelette (using up leftovers from the week's cooking), Smothered Fresh Sausage, and homemade biscuits with Fig Preserves.

By now you know what a fuss we like to make over holiday meals. For Thanksgiving, our feast might include:

Smoked *or* Deep-Fried Turkey
Cajun Rice Dressing
Cornbread Dressing
Maque Choux
Sweet Potato Casserole with Praline Topping
Petits Pois
Assorted Sweets

At Christmastime, we go even further:

Baked Whole Fresh Pork Ham
Cajun Rice Dressing
Stuffed Tomatoes
Smothered Snap Beans

Cajun Eggplant Dressing
Maque Choux
Divinity
Russian Rocks
Ice Box Cookies
Pralines

For a wedding reception or other large gathering, we like to prepare a sumptuous, colorful buffet. It might include:

Cheese Straws
Daube Glacé
Cajun Pâté
Marinated Crab Fingers
Hot Crab Dip
Seafood Mold
Shrimp Rémoulade
Smoked Turkey
Molded Chicken Salad

Sometimes we like to create the occasion for a big feast—a favorite excuse is an open house. Everyone drops by and helps himself to the buffet, which in summertime would include something like this:

Marinated Crab Fingers
Shrimp Rémoulade
Assorted Pickles
Corn and Crab Bisque
Shrimp Ms. Ann
Molded Chicken Salad
Sliced Home-Grown Tomatoes
Cheese Straws
Fresh Strawberries in Cream
Pineapple Upside-Down Cake

In wintertime, our open-house offerings are a little heartier:

> Daube Glacé
> Cajun Pâté
> Oyster Stew
> Hot Crab Dip
> Seafood Mold
> Roasted Pecans
> Duck and Sausage Gumbo
> Boudin
> Smothered Sausage
> Smoked Turkey
> Fudge
> Pralines
> Old Dominion Pound Cake
> Pecan Pie

All these lively flavors obviously call for beverages with character. We're fond of hard liquor—bourbon, scotch, and mixed drinks like bloody marys or mimosas, especially. A full-bodied red wine is an excellent complement to most Cajun dinners—my restaurant reserve is a California cabernet sauvignon—and a bold white is nice, too. Iced tea and lemonade are good nonalcoholic drinks for our climate. Beer? Anytime, anyplace.

Sources

If you learn any one thing from this book, I hope it's that a cook's greatest strength is in knowing how to make the most of what's around him. But every now and again, you may want to try a Cajun specialty for which you just can't get the ingredients locally. The Louisiana Seafood Promotion Board can provide you free of charge with a complete list of seafood processors in the state who will ship fresh seafood. Write them at P.O. Box 15570, Baton Rouge, LA 70895, or telephone them at (504) 383-7710.

Here are a few excellent suppliers of seafood and special Louisiana products:

Bon Creole Seafood
Route 3
Box 5180
New Iberia, LA 70560
Telephone: (318) 229-8397
Fresh and frozen crawfish and crawfish fat

Catfish Wholesale
P.O. Box 759
Abbeville, LA 70510
Telephone: (318) 643-6700
Fresh catfish, saltwater fish, crawfish, crab meat, alligator

C. J.'s
Route 1
Box 1416
Breaux Bridge, LA 70517
Telephone: (318) 845-4413
Crawfish

Harlon's
P.O. Box 1287
Metairie, LA 70004
Telephone: (504) 831-4592
All kinds of seafood, fresh and frozen

Batistella's
1919 Touro Street
New Orleans, LA 70116
Telephone: (504) 949-2724
All kinds of seafood, fresh and frozen

Louisiana Cajun Seafood
P.O. Box 806
Abbeville, LA 70511
Telephone: (318) 898-9651
Crab meat, crawfish, and oysters

K-Paul's
500 Mandeville Street
New Orleans, LA 70117
Telephone: (800) 654-6107
Tasso and andouille

❧ INDEX ❧

ABOUT THE AUTHOR

Alex Patout was born and raised in New Iberia, Louisiana, where since 1979 he and his family have operated Patout's. The family recently opened a second restaurant in Los Angeles, and a third on St. Charles Avenue in New Orleans.